WHAT OTHERS ARE SAYING

"Numbers matter. They matter on paychecks, score-boards, medical charts, and speedometers; and, *Faith by Numbers* makes clear, they should matter to Christians. Without playing annoyingly cute games with numbers or mnemonics, Eichinger shows us why numbers matter for the simple walk of faith and the ongoing task of catechizing the saints. This short book weaves together animated narrative accounts, numeric rhythms of Scripture, and foundational doctrinal truth in an engaging and rewarding way that will benefit every disciple of Christ."

—Rev. Dr. Joel Biermann
Professor of Systematic Theology, Concordia Seminary, St. Louis, and author of *A Case for Character* and *Wholly Citizens*.

"Pastor Eichinger has produced a helpful book that will be appreciated by anyone who is interested in resources for Bible study, whether in a pastor's study or a small group setting. Eric has a wonderful way with words, and is able to convey important theological concepts in a faithful and easy to understand fashion. This is a wonderful resource."

—Pastor Tim Seeber
Zion Lutheran Church, Kalamazoo, MI

"Anyone who's ever read Scripture has noticed that certain numbers repeat themselves. And any pastor who has taught a Bible class has had someone ask about the significance of these numbers. Rev. Eichinger's work brings faithful, grace-filled clarity to these numbers. Eichinger tackles the numbers in Scripture from the unique perspective of the Six Chief Parts of Luther's Small Catechism and uses the repeating numbers of Scripture to teach God's children His grace, mercy, and love. This book is a must have for every catechist's shelf."

—Rev. Ross Engel
Host of the *Ringside Preachers* podcast, Author at *The Jagged Word*, Navy Chaplain, and Senior Pastor of St. Peter's Lutheran Church, Middleburg, FL

"If you have ever wondered about the significance of numbers in Scripture, this book sums it up nicely! Pastor Eric Eichinger has produced a handy little primer on biblical numerology from a strong confessional Lutheran perspective that speaks to catechetical students of all ages. *Faith by Numbers* provides a tremendous opportunity and great clarity to a deeper understanding of God's powerful Word."

—Rev. Dr. Gregory S. Walton
President, Florida–Georgia District, LCMS

"These pages, brimming with creativity and fidelity, will enable teachers and students of the Bible to truly "count their blessings." As number after number is mined for its biblical significance, we learn to count our blessings and enumerate the ways that God works in our lives. By the end, all those tens, threes, sevens, and other numbers scattered through the Scriptures, and expressed in the teachings of the Catechism, will shed light on all the gifts we have in Jesus Christ."

—Chad Bird
Author and Scholar in Residence at 1517.org

"We live in a world of numbers and counting. We count our age, assets, and various anniversaries, all for the purpose of tracking and making sense of the dimensions of our lives. Pastor Eichinger gives us a closer look at the numbers intentionally weaved throughout Scripture. Thoughtfully he brings the message and themes of God's love through Christ Jesus into view through the common and not so common numerical texts in Scripture. *Faith by Numbers* provides an organized catechetical work by which to better understand the dimensions of our lives within the principles of faith."

—Dr. Michael Walcheski
Associate Vice President, Professor of Psychology & Family Science, Concordia St. Paul, MN

"The repetitive use of numbers in the Holy Scriptures is not thoughtless or inconsequential. Eric Eichinger does a masterful job of explaining this and showing how the weaving together of numbers and theological truths is an important feature of how the Scriptures speak to us. Eichinger's capturing of these biblical design patterns and subsequent flushing out their relevance for the modern reader is a much-needed resource for God's people."

—Todd A. Stryd, PsyD, MDiv
Philadelphia, PA

Susan,

you ARE #1 in My Book!! ;)

Faith by Numbers

DECIPHERING DOCTRINE
WITH BIBLICAL NUMEROLOGY

Eric T. Eichinger

love, Eric Eichinger 5/22

CrossLink Publishing
RAPID CITY, SD

Eichinger/CrossLink Publishing
1601 Mt. Rushmore Rd., Ste 3288
Rapid City, SD 57701
www.CrossLinkPublishing.com

Faith by Numbers / Eric T. Eichinger. —1st ed.
ISBN 978-1-63357-390-1
Library of Congress Control Number: 2021933624

To my parents,

David & Carol Eichinger,

who taught me innumerable values of the faith.

CONTENTS

FOREWORD

We all react slowly to imperceptible changes in culture, and we have had many in recent decades. Most people sense things have changed in America and the world, the changes leaving them disoriented and anxious, but they can't put a finger on what has happened. Scholarly observers, not all but many, do understand the changes but their academic insights do not reach people too busy with the day staring at them, people trying to make ends meet, people yearning for better relationships, gullible people believing traditional and social media or the opposite, people filled with distrust and cynicism about almost everything. Is there a bridge to bring insight, and for religious people God's truth, to give focus and help to our fellow citizens? One bridge is pastoral ministry. Like all of us, theologians see cultural changes in hindsight, but biblical theologians make a unique contribution by assessing decadal changes through faith and encouraging with the bright hope of God's future.

Early on, Eric Eichinger identifies a significant shift in biblical interpreters. "Attempting to connect biblical numerology to specific doctrinal tenets exudes more than a whiff of skepticism for any good Christian scholar." That sentence touches something extremely important. A

1

result of the Enlightenment has been rigorous and rational exegetical study of biblical texts, but now postmodernism, our post-churched era, sees more than academics in presenting Bible truths. Interpretation is also formational, asking not only what the text communicated in its original setting but how the Spirit of God works to form his people today. "The Word of God is not interpreted; it interprets" (Fred Craddock, "As One Without Authority," 35). The Enlightenment dismissed the figurative interpretation of the church fathers but figurative presentation is reclaiming respectability among Christians who see faith formation needing more than historical analysis of old texts. Pastor Eichinger asks, "Is there something more going on here than the first layer of the text?" Indeed there is.

The point is that we live in the present, and the formation of the Christian believer is the Spirit's work today through the texts of the Word. The great advocate of *sola scriptura*, Martin Luther, knew there are times to set aside the purely intellectual to let the Spirit form us here-and-now through the prompts of the Word. About the Lord's Prayer, Luther wrote, "I do stay as close as possible to the thoughts and content. It happens often that in my meditation I come across such rich thoughts, that I disregard the other six petitions. When such a wealth of ideas comes, one should forego other petitions and make room for such thoughts, listen silently...." When *Faith by Numbers* may seem to bring unrelated texts together, ponder, not in academic analysis but with heart for the furthering formation of your faith. "Under these conditions the Holy Spirit is preaching and in his sermon one word is better than a thousand in our prayer. I have learned much more

from this kind of listening than I could have from much
reading and reflection."

—Rev. Dr. Dale A. Meyer
Emeritus President, Concordia Seminary, St. Louis

INTRODUCTION

"And the LORD took him outside and said, 'Now look to the heavens and count the stars, if you are able.' Then He told him, 'So shall your offspring be.' Abram believed the LORD, and it was credited to him as righteousness" (Genesis 15:5–6).

God used the concept of counting the number of stars to teach Abram how many descendants would come after him in the faith—and Abram's faith was credited to him as righteousness. The power of numbers is exponential, particularly when God uses them to teach. God's Word did not return void. Abram's descendants in the faith have multiplied and expanded, grafting in gentile believers, including Christians of all stripes.

The Bible is a bottomless well of knowledge. While our minds are finite, God's mind is infinite. His endless truth is ever before us, embedded in the Word of His Scriptures, but it can appear daunting to investigate. Consequently, many passages of the Scriptures are not frequently read, or properly understood. Yet, countless realizations are waiting to be discovered, every day.

For instance, there are several reoccurring themes God uses throughout the Bible, that are fascinating when examined in depth. One of these themes is how God seemingly attaches meaning to numbers—specific numbers. How those numbers are used in context subtly accentuate some of God's major teachings throughout the entirety of the Scriptures. The intention of this book is to reinforce the foundational bedrock of our Christian faith by exploring some of the beautiful Biblical theology woven within the usage of numbers, and the often-unrecognized meanings behind them. Martin Luther, and his catechetical zeal for teaching the family, will occasionally serve as luminary escort as well as some of our Early Church Fathers.

It should be noted that our early Christian Church Fathers rejected the Gnostic (secret knowledge) concepts of understanding numbers mystically, as to possess a metaphysical importance in and of themselves. Irenaeus once said:

> "[The Gnostics] endeavor to bring forward proof [of their system] through means of numbers, and the syllables of names, sometimes also through the letters of syllables, and yet again through those numbers, which are according to the practice followed by the Greeks, contained in different letters: this, I say, demonstrates in the clearest manner of their overthrow and confusion, as well as the untenable and perverse character of their professed knowledge. However, some believed that

certain numbers in the Bible could be understood symbolically, pointing to higher truths."[1]

While St. Irenaeus remained a harsh critic of the Gnostic system of mystical numerology, he did not conclude that their numerological analysis is a fallacious thing in itself. Justin Martyr once even went so far as to quote Pythagoras when he defended the belief in monotheism. Many of the Church Fathers recognized symbolic value of Biblical numbers, and that occasionally they can indeed point toward *higher truths*.

Certainly, attempting to connect Biblical numerology to specific doctrinal tenets exudes more than a whiff of skepticism for any good Christian scholar. This book is *not* about indiscriminately using random numbers in attempts to produce some type of *Bible code* pathway to secret enlightenment. Nor does it invent Sunday school parlor games utilizing chapter and verse numbers to satisfy its theological exploits. Rather, this book explores well-acquainted truths of God's word, within prominent passages as well as less familiar numeric text references, and practically associates them to our well-known teachings of the Christian faith. The aftermath will expand our biblical appreciation of catechesis, entrenched in the Scriptures, and ideally help the reader commit them deeper into memory.

There are several numbers in the Bible that recur with great significance. New and seasoned readers of the Bible do not always recognize all of these instances, or their

---

1. Saint Irenaeus, *Against Heretics*, Book II.

underlying meanings. More often than not there is a rich-er second-level textual reading attached to these num-bers. Numbers referenced in the Bible do not *always* car-ry a secondary or tertiary theological relevance in their respective contexts, yet when and where those numbers are recorded, we owe ourselves as faithful Christian scholars to at least ask the question, "Is there something more going on here than the first layer of the text?"

Six of the most common numbers that stand out are: 3, 7, 8, 10, 12, and 40. Each of these numbers specifi-cally and consistently convey profound meaning as they are frequently referenced throughout the Scriptures. When these numbers and themes are cross-referenced with some of our rich Christian dogma, a helpful pattern emerges and can help reinforce our basic doctrinal con-fession of faith:

Three (Trinitarian) associates quite fittingly to the three articles of the Apostles' Creed.

Seven (Perfection) conveniently connects to the seven petitions of the Lord's Prayer, which the disciples asked that Christ teach them how to pray.

Eight (Promise/Covenant) connotes baptism and eighth day theology.

Ten (Completion/Judgment) readily links to the Ten Commandments.

Twelve (The Church) alludes to the Lord's Supper, where, notably, the twelve were gathered when Christ in-stituted the meal for His Church.

Forty (Testing and Hope) relates to confession and ab-solution, and the waiting/suffering the sinner agonizes through the process of confessing sin—ultimately leading to the sinner/saint, forgiven by Christ's grace, the new hope of salvation, and an end to suffering.

These six numbers and their multiples pop up frequently, and often thematically, in their respective contexts to their doctrinal counterparts. Interpretation can at times play a controversial role in the realm of theology and Christian doctrine. Anytime particular biblical words, verses, or passages are translated there is potential for disagreement. Each word in the biblical text serves as a *signifier*, whereas the *conceptual signified* in each reader's mind might vary, potentially leaving room for different opinions. It doesn't take much for an opposing armchair theologian to offer a hot take interpretation, which invariably results in heated debate. Biblical number references, on the other hand, are also signifiers, yet the conceptual signifieds remain uniform by every reader. Numbers cannot be translated any other way and are the same in every tongue, tribe, and nation.

If the Tower of Babel taught humanity anything, it's that multiple variant languages cause confusion. However, counting and number patterns cut through cultural and language barriers with ease. God created the concept of numbers and counting in the very first week of creation. Numbers are essentially the universal language. It would seem only fitting that God could also communicate to us, and even teach us, our faith by numbers.

THE NUMBER THREE

3

"The third time's the charm" is an old adage invoked enough times in the present age that it warrants an entry into the pop culture urban dictionary. There is something about the number three. To some, *three* is circumstantial to mystical reasoning, said to explain why mysterious events might implausibly occur in a series of three. Comedy also loves to employ the use of three. It is the unspoken rule with reoccurring jokes; three is golden, four is overkill, (five is right out)! The number three certainly possesses an enchanting quality. One might even say, divine.

Biblically speaking the number three tends to suggest a trinitarian emphasis. This chapter will survey the various occurrences of the number three in the Scriptures. It will also make note how three often accentuates the presence of the trinity in the biblical narrative, and why this can help us remember the three articles of the Apostles' Creed.

The fact that the word *Trinity* is never used in the Bible is frequently volleyed across the theological debate stage as to somehow diminish the triune nature of the Christian God. This is no exposed divine dilemma. Quite simply, *Trinity* is theological shorthand terminology for Christians to concisely speak of their faith in the Father (Creator), the Son (Redeemer), and the Spirit (Sanctifier), without incessant long-winded references amid conversation.

The triune nature of one God in three persons is mentioned throughout the Bible, directly and indirectly. Look no further than the first three verses of Genesis.

> "In the beginning, God created the heavens and the earth. The earth was without form and void, and darkness was over the face of the deep. And the Spirit of God was hovering over the face of the waters. And God said, 'Let there be light,' and there was light" (Genesis 1:1–3).

In this passage, God the Father reigns without question, but there is also reference of the Spirit as well as the spoken *Word* of God. If God has a voice, it is Christ's. John chapter one further clarifies that Christ is indeed *the Word* of God made flesh. Moreover, the Hebrew language consistently uses the Word for God in plural form. The great Reformer, Martin Luther, had a fair amount to say about this:

> "...the word, 'Let Us make' is aimed at making sure the mystery of our faith, by which we believe that from eternity there is one God and that there are three separate Persons in one Godhead: the Father,

the Son, and the Holy Spirit. The Jews indeed try in various ways to get around this passage, but they advance nothing sound against it. Moreover, Luther states, 'Let Us make', and 'He made,' in the plural and in the singular; thereby Moses clearly and forcibly shows us that within and in the very Godhead and the Creating Essence there is one inseparable and eternal plurality." And, "But, you say, these evidences are too dark to prove so important an article of faith. I answer: At that time these statements had to be made so darkly by divine counsel, or at least because all things were reserved for that future Lord for whose arrival was reserved the restitution of all things (Acts 3:21) , of all knowledge, and of all revelations... and yet the holy Patriarchs had this knowledge through the Holy Spirit, although not with such clarity as now, when we hear mentioned in the New Testament the Father, the Son, and the Holy Spirit."[2]

Scriptural evidence for the Trinity is ubiquitous. There are further trinitarian undertones in creation with reference to space, time, and matter. Fascinatingly, each of those three fields of creation reveal three more trinities within a trinity. Concerning space; there is length, width, and height, within time; past, present, and future,

2. Plass, *What Luther Says*, P.1522

and regarding matter; solid, liquid, and gas. The fingerprints of the one true, yet triune God; Father, Son, and Holy Spirit, are literally everywhere within His creation where we dwell.

The Bible provides many divine trinitarian reference-examples to learn from as well. Following are but three different New Testament personalities writing about the Trinity:

Paul writes:

> "For through Him [Jesus] we both have access in one Spirit to the Father" (Ephesians 2:18). And, "In Him [Jesus] you also are being built together into a dwelling place for God by the Spirit" (Ephesians 2:22).

The author of Hebrews states,

> "How much more will the blood of Christ, who through the eternal Spirit offered himself without blemish to God, purify our conscience from dead works to serve the living God" (Hebrews 9:14).

One of Jesus' disciples concludes his Gospel with,

> "Go therefore and make disciples of all nations, baptizing them in the name of the Father and of the Son and of the Holy Spirit" (Matthew 28:19).

Explaining the Trinity is an impossibly infinite task with no satisfying answer for mortal finite minds. No analogy ever measures up, as one cannot "confuse the persons or divide the substance."[3] We feel compelled to explain things, thereby possessing the knowledge, but the Trinity is mysteriously elusive in a way that keeps us coming back to learn more. Attempting to explain the Trinity is more like meddling with a million-sided Rubik's Cube, with matching color variants for each side. We pick it up to fuss with and be fascinated for a time, only to set it down in perplexed vexation, again and again. So goes attempting to explain the Trinity. The Trinity is not some simple concept to be processed. All the while God wants to be the focus of our perpetual attention.

Martin Luther believed that we should not dispute about the Trinity, for it is by its very nature beyond all reason, but it should be enough for us that God speaks in this way about Himself and reveals Himself thus in His Word. "Who can understand anything about these things by means of reason?"[4]

Rather than explain, Christians humbly and purely proclaim God's story via His revealed identity. Therefore, to speak of God is to proclaim His name. To say who God is, is to confess what He does. Over the course of Christendom, creeds were written to aid Christians to concisely proclaim their faith. Suitably, there are three ecumenical creeds. The Apostles' Creed is the oldest and shortest, followed by the Nicene Creed, and finally the lengthy Athanasian Creed. That loquaciously long creed

---

3. The Athanasian Creed
4. Martin Luther, *Table Talk* p.378.

is customarily only brought out one Sunday per year for a congregation to laboriously recite on, no surprise: Trinity Sunday. The lengthiness of each creed grew over the years as more doctrinal specificity needed to be clarified for enquiring minds.

The creeds of faith used by Christians encapsulates the biblical doctrine of the Trinity and phrases it in a welcoming way. Much like the three-act structure of storytelling is helpful for how humans process information, the identity of the Trinity, as articulated in the Christian creeds, flow similarly. Each creed is aptly made up of three articles, specifically addressing the nature of each person in the Godhead of the Trinity. By proclaiming who each person is in the Trinity: Father, Son, and Holy Spirit, we declare what each person does: Creator, Redeemer, and Sanctifier, respectively, and thereby, tell the glory story of Christ whenever the Christian faith is confessed.

Saint Timothy describes the cryptic wrestling with identity of God as such:

> "Great indeed, we confess, is the mystery of godliness: He was manifested in the flesh, vindicated by the Spirit, seen by angels, proclaimed among the nations, believed on in the world, taken up in glory" (1 Timothy 3:16).

Originally, God walked and talked in the presence of Adam in the Garden of Eden, but that did not seem to last long. Sin and the fall of humanity set in. Mankind's intimate interface with God ceased and became more nebulous than ever imaginable. God, and His Trinitarian identity, hence, has been riddled with mystery from mankind's vantage point. The world and the Church continue to fixate about the Trinity for all of life, ever fascinated, never fully comprehending, yet firmly confessing by faith. God, however, would provide His clues along the way for the world to know who He is.

+++

The first article of the Apostles' Creed is about God the Father, the first person of the Trinity, and His work of creation. Christians learn to confess, "I believe in God, the Father Almighty, maker of heaven and earth."

God doesn't just enjoy walking and talking in the midst of his creation, He also seems to relish hanging out with His creation. God did so with Adam before sin entered creation. Consequently, God desires all people to be saved and works to restore mankind's relationship with Him. In a one-of-a-kind divine manifestation, God appears to reveal Himself in the form of three men, and begins to put in motion His eventual plans for redemption.

The gift of life is arguably the biggest aspect to appreciate in God the Father's creative activity. Abraham serves as a prime example of coming to appreciate the gift of life. He would learn in a painfully hard way what becoming the father of many nations would mean, long after God made that promise to him.

> "The Lord appeared to Abraham near the great trees of Mamre while he was sitting at the entrance to his tent in the heat of the day. Abraham looked up and saw three

men standing nearby. When he saw them,
he hurried from the entrance of his tent to
meet them and bowed low to the ground.
He said, 'If I have found favor in your eyes,
my lord, do not pass your servant by. Let
a little water be brought, and then you
may all wash your feet and rest under this
tree. Let me get you something to eat, so
you can be refreshed and then go on your
way—now that you have come to your servant'" (Genesis 18:1–5).

The exact identity of the three visitors is curious to say
the least. The Hebrew text demonstrates this peculiarity
via a healthy dose of interplay between plural and singular pronouns throughout the context of the three visitors.
At minimum, this physical appearance is a strong suggestion that the Trinity is a threefold character of God's
personhood.

These three visitors of Abraham walked with him,
talked with him, and even ate food prepared by Sarah.
The relaxed conversational scene plays out much like
Jesus interacting with His disciples, even including a bit
of humor in the exchange. The three visitors soon prepare
to depart but not before they make their biggest contribution of their visitation. Preposterously, they reiterate
an earlier promise from God that Sarah—with an elderly
barren womb—will indeed give birth to a son.

Stop me if you've heard this one before.

Sarah evidently hadn't and could not help but gig-
gle as she eavesdropped over the seemingly fake news.
Abraham looked awkwardly at the straight faces of the

three visitors after Sarah laughed. Imaginatively the crickets were loud in that moment.

> Then the LORD said to Abraham, "Why did Sarah laugh and say, 'Will I really have a child, now that I am old?' Is anything too hard for the LORD? I will return to you at the appointed time next year, and Sarah will have a son." Sarah was afraid, so she lied and said, "I did not laugh." But he said, "Yes, you did laugh" (Genesis 18:13–15).

Tough crowd. The three visitors did not apparently see the humor in what they had said, but Sarah did. The idea that she would finally, in extreme old age, have a son to advance their legacy was foolishly comical.

Here the Trinity does what the Trinity does—impart the Gospel. The Father sends the Son, with the Spirit equipping hearers to believe. St. Paul would later offer insight upon the apparently absurd attempt of believing in God's promise in the face of a disbelieving world:

> "For the message of the cross is foolishness to those who are perishing, but to us who are being saved it is the power of God" (1 Corinthians 1:19).

If Sarah's situation induces a snicker, wait till you hear the one about a virgin who will give birth to a son.

The three visitors remained stoic. They knew the son from Sarah's barren womb foreshadowed the miraculous Son of Mary's virgin womb, and that Son would indeed "rest under a tree" in a different capacity. Yet only the devil would be laughing at that ghastly punchline.

+++

The second article of the Apostles' Creed concerns Christ Jesus, the second person of the Trinity, and how He works justification.

> "And in Jesus Christ, His only Son, our Lord, who was conceived by the Holy Spirit, born of the Virgin Mary, suffered under Pontius Pilate, was crucified, died and was buried. He descended into hell. The third day He rose again from the dead. He ascended into heaven and sits at the right hand of God, the Father Almighty. From thence He will come to judge the living and the dead."

The redeeming nature of Christ would not have been possible if not for the fact that Jesus died and rose again from the dead. Jesus is the firstborn of the dead and is the source of justification via His death and resurrection. He justifies us before God the Father by the shedding of His holy, precious, and innocent blood.

Marvelously, the Father, the Son, and the Spirit each get an assist on the play that is Christ's resurrection; The Father's work is mentioned, "*and you killed the Author of life, whom God raised from the dead*" (Acts 3:15). Jesus refers to his body as the temple when he declares, "*Destroy this temple, and in three days I will raise it up*" (John

FAITH BY NUMBERS • 21

10:17–18). The role of the Holy Spirit is also referenced by Saint Paul, *"and was declared to be the Son of God in power according to the Spirit of holiness by his resurrection from the dead"* (Romans 1:4).

The Trinity is vital to the resurrection. So, when the prophet Elijah was used by God to foreshadow this important aspect of the faith, it is no surprise that the number three turns up in a most unique way.

"After this the son of the woman, the mistress of the house, became ill. And his illness was so severe that there was no breath left in him. And she said to Elijah, "What have you against me, O man of God? You have come to me to bring my sin to remembrance and to cause the death of my son!" And he said to her, "Give me your son." And he took him from her arms and carried him up into the upper chamber where he lodged, and laid him on his own bed. And he cried to the Lord, "O Lord my God, have you brought calamity even upon the widow with whom I sojourn, by killing her son?" Then he stretched himself upon the child three times and cried to the Lord, "O Lord my God, let this child's life come into him again." And the Lord listened to the voice of Elijah. And the life of the child came into him again, and he revived. And Elijah took the child and brought him down from the upper chamber into the house and delivered him

to his mother. And Elijah said, "See, your
son lives." And the woman said to Elijah,
"Now I know that you are a man of God,
and that the word of the Lord in your
mouth is truth" (1 Kings 17:17–24).

Just when hope begins to emerge in the land due to
Elijah's present proclamation, the widow feels the crippling sting of death in the loss of her son. Elijah, a prophet whose ministry was marked by intense prayer and
response from God, performs the impossible. He raises
the widow's son back to life. Intriguingly, not until he
stretches out over the boy in prayer three times does the
boy breathe life again.

The Triune God is ever near, particularly in resurrection work. While remaining unseen, this subtle inclusion
of a threefold prayer serves as one more mildly suggestive allusion of the Trinity's constant presence throughout the Old Testament.[5]

+++

The third article of the Apostles' Creed pertains to the
Holy Spirit, the third person of the Trinity, and sanctification: how He makes us holy. "I believe in the Holy Spirit,
the holy catholic church, the communion of saints, the
forgiveness of sins, the resurrection of the body, and the
life everlasting." The work of the Holy Spirit is invisible,

---

5. Lessing, *Jonah*, p.190 "The OT uses the number three slightly
more often than the number seven. An act is repeated three times to
enhance it or bring it to consummation."

equipping the nonbeliever to actually believe in God and His Word and wonders.

Another Old Testament prophet, Jonah, would function as another Trinitarian conduit of grace. Jonah had considerably less enthusiasm than pretty much any prophet, of all time, ever.

Jonah detested the idea of the Ninevites coming to faith in God. He bitterly loathed the situation so much he actually ran from the Lord's task of preaching to them. No matter, the Triune Lord had a different mouthwatering method of getting Jonah's attention. Meanwhile, Jonah distressingly told the sailors to throw him overboard to appease the wrath of God for his disobedience.

God showed up in a most unusual way. "And the LORD appointed a great fish to swallow up Jonah. And Jonah was in the belly of the fish three days and three nights" (Jonah 1:17). A man doesn't spend three days in the belly of the whale without having a revelation or two. Jonah finally realized that there was nowhere he could go to escape the call of God's Word. After Jonah prays and returns to God's word, the whale coughed him up onto dry land. The Lord spoke to him "Arise, go to Nineveh, that great city, and call out against it the message that I tell you" (Jonah 3:2).

"Arise." The Triune Lord speaks resurrection language to Jonah in order for him to proclaim God's Word to those who need to hear it. All the persons of the Trinity are once again at work. It might appear merely coincidental that Jonah spent three days in the belly of the fish, only to burst forth on the third day, restored in newness of life and forgiveness.

Jesus didn't think so.

"For just as Jonah was three days and three nights in the belly of the great fish, so will the Son of Man be three days and three nights in the heart of the earth. The men of Nineveh will rise up at the judgment with this generation and condemn it, for they repented at the preaching of Jonah, and behold, something greater than Jonah is here." (Matthew 12:40–41).

God chased Jonah to the depths of Sheol and plucked him out. He wanted him to preach His Word, that the Spirit would equip nonbelievers to repent and believe.[6]

Something greater than Jonah is indeed here, and that something is Jesus Christ.

+++

"And when Jesus was baptized, immediately he went up from the water, and behold, the heavens were opened to him, and he saw the Spirit of God descending like a dove and coming to rest on him; and behold, a voice from heaven said, "This

---

6. Lessing, *Jonah* p.204. "Three days (and three nights)" can be the length of a journey. Sometimes the journey is more mundane (e.g., Gen 30:36), but in other passages, including the narrative of Israel's exodus redemption, the goal of a journey of three days is the worship of Yahweh, the true God. If this interpretation is correct, the "three days and three nights" in Jonah 2:1 is the period of time it takes the great fish to bring Jonah back from Sheol and the brink of death to life and the worship of Yahweh."

is my beloved Son, with whom I am well pleased" (Matthew 3:16–17).

Christ's unity within the Trinity is an innate aspect to His personhood as fully divine and simultaneously fully human. Jesus is the embodiment of the perfect miraculous mystery.[7] That being stated, it is curious that Jesus established a trio of disciples within the twelve. Throughout the Gospels, Jesus consistently gravitates toward Peter, James, and John, and occasionally imparted specific revelations to that inner circle.

There are fittingly three particular instances when Jesus takes aside Peter, James, and John from the rest. The first occurrence was when Jairus's daughter had died, in Matthew chapter five. They were present in the room when Jesus raised the girl back to life. The second time is when Jesus revealed His divine identity to them (in the presence of Moses and Elijah) at the Mount of Transfiguration in Matthew chapter seventeen. The third excursion was to the Garden of Gethsemane in Matthew chapter twenty-six. Jesus invited Peter, James, and John to accompany Him in prayer as He faced His hour of suffering to come.

Each instance dovetails well with the primary work of the Trinity and gives credence to the three articles of faith; Creation and the regifting of life, the nature of

---

7. Kolb and Wengert, *The Book of Concord* P.512. "Christ is and remains for all eternity God and human being in one inseparable person, which is the highest mystery after the mystery of the Holy Trinity, as the Apostle testifies [1 Timothy 3:16]. In this mystery lie our only comfort, life, and salvation."

Christ fulfilling the Law and the Prophets, and the sanc-
tifying role of prayer and keeping the faith during dark
times. Notably, Christ's disciples witness Jesus's ministry
and teaching in their presence for three years.

Paul of Tarsus, who wrote the majority of the New
Testament, was not part of the original twelve disciples
of Christ. However, he too studied for three years soon
after his roadside conversion to Christianity.

> "But when he who had set me apart be-
> fore I was born, and who called me by
> his grace, was pleased to reveal his Son
> to me, in order that I might preach him
> among the Gentiles, I did not immediately
> consult with anyone, nor did I go up to
> Jerusalem to those who were apostles be-
> fore me, but I went away into Arabia, and
> returned again to Damascus. Then after
> three years I went up to Jerusalem to visit
> Cephas and remained with him fifteen
> days" (Galatians 1:15–18).

Paul would go on to write the majority of the New
Testament, with plenty of theological jewels to mine like
this one:

> "Now there are varieties of gifts, but the
> same Spirit; and there are varieties of ser-
> vice, but the same Lord; and there are va-
> rieties of activities, but it is the same God

FAITH BY NUMBERS • 27

who empowers them all in everyone" (1 Corinthians 12:4–6).[8]

Well before Paul would attend his exclusive three-year seminary-like experience, Peter would have to endure his hardest lesson about God, threefold.

The stage was set. The plot to kill Jesus was in motion. The last supper was still being digested when Jesus prompted His disciples with a heartburning matter: They would all fall away from Him that very night. This did not sit well with Peter.

> "Peter answered him, "Though they all fall away because of you, I will never fall away." Jesus said to him, "Truly, I tell you, this very night, before the rooster crows, you will deny me three times" (Matthew 26:33–34).

To deny Christ is to deny God, which is essentially to deny the Triune God. To that end it is thought-provoking that Jesus tells Peter he will deny Him exactly three times before the following morning. It is remarkable that Peter would contest Jesus in this way. Peter had witnessed more than enough to know better than doubt His words at this point. Regardless, never bet on one's self, when the alternative is Christ. Jesus will call that bluff every time.

---

8. Lockwood, 1 Corinthians p.420 "There can be no doubt that Paul in 12:4–6 is giving expression to what later became known as the Christian doctrine of the Trinity: "Spirit,... Lord... God." As has been well said, here we have an important part of the Pauline "stuff" from which the Trinitarian doctrine was later formulated."

One might as well bring a knife to a gunfight, which is basically what Peter did next.

Jesus and the disciples gathered at the Mount of Olives. Jesus asked His followers to keep watch and pray as He withdrew to pray. "Father, if you are willing, remove this cup from me. Nevertheless, not my will, but yours, be done" (Luke 22:42). Jesus returned to His disciples only to find them sleeping. He woke them and repeated the process and prayer a total of three times until Judas arrived with the lynch posse. The half-light of the moon was just bright enough for Judas to identify Jesus to the soldiers with a betraying kiss. Peter drew his sword and struck the ear of one of the men. Jesus rebuked Peter, instructing that He must drink the cup His Father has given Him to drink. Then the soldiers led Jesus away.

As Jesus predicted, all the disciples fled and fell away from Him. To Peter's credit, he was still on the fringe of faithfulness, lurking in the shadows. The furthest thought from Peter's mind was how Jesus's painful prophecy would soon play out in triplicate.

> Now Peter was sitting outside in the courtyard. And a servant girl came up to him and said, "You also were with Jesus the Galilean." But he denied it before them all, saying, "I do not know what you mean." And when he went out to the entrance, another servant girl saw him, and she said to the bystanders, "This man was with Jesus of Nazareth." And again he denied it with an oath: "I do not know the man." After a little while the bystanders came up

and said to Peter, "Certainly you too are
one of them, for your accent betrays you."
Then he began to invoke a curse on himself and to swear, "I do not know the man."
And immediately the rooster crowed. And
Peter remembered the saying of Jesus,
"Before the rooster crows, you will deny
me three times." And he went out and
wept bitterly (Matthew 26:69–75).

Jesus had to die, to pay for the sins of the world. It was
by divine appointment, and God's timing would again be
noteworthy. "It was the third hour when they crucified
Him." Mark (15:25). Jesus was placed on the cross at the
third hour of the day (9 a.m.) and died at the ninth hour
(3 p.m.). There were also three hours of darkness that
covered the land while Jesus was suffering on the cross
from the sixth hour to the ninth hour, until Christ gave
up his spirit.

On the Third Day

Jesus lay dead over the course of three days, Friday,
Saturday, and into Sunday morning. He was unequivo-
cally deceased. The Roman soldiers saw to that fact. They
were experts at inflicting death, as painfully as possible.
Then something miraculous happened. Something that
changed the world with eternal permanence. Death was
swallowed up in victory.

The resurrection on the third day had been prophesied
in the Old Testament and reiterated by Christ Himself on

more than one occasion.[9] God had been very clear. On the third day He would bring everything to fulfillment. And God upheld His Word as He raised Jesus on, of all days, the third day. The goal of the Trinity, the glory story came to fruition: creation, redemption, and sanctification. Peter was relieved to hear the trifold emphasized news.

> When they had finished breakfast, Jesus said to Simon Peter, "Simon, son of John, do you love me more than these?" He said to him, "Yes, Lord; you know that I love you." He said to him, "Feed my lambs." He said to him a second time, "Simon, son of John, do you love me?" He said to him, "Yes, Lord; you know that I love you." He said to him, "Tend my sheep." He said to him the third time, "Simon, son of John, do you love me?" Peter was grieved because he said to him the third time, "Do you love me?" and he said to him, "Lord, you know everything; you know that I love you." Jesus said to him, "Feed my sheep. Truly, truly, I say to you, when you were young, you used to dress yourself and

9. Just, *Luke*, p.557, "There is a close relationship between Lk 13:32–35 and Luke 24, especially in the time reference in Luke 13.32. "and on the third day I am brought to my goal," another proleptic demonstration during the ministry of Jesus of the eschatological fulfillment of Jesus work on Easter, the third day as recorded in Luke 24 that illustrates the crucial role Luke 13 plays in Luke's thematic development."

> walk wherever you wanted, but when you
> are old, you will stretch out your hands,
> and another will dress you and carry you
> where you do not want to go." (This he
> said to show by what kind of death he was
> to glorify God.) And after saying this he
> said to him, "Follow me" (John 21:15–19).

Jesus reinstated Peter, as He reinstates all believers, ashamed by their sin. His word of gospel comfort forgives and heals for us today as much as it did for Peter then. Peter's confession of faith would be foundational for the church. Peter would also join the other New Testament writers who testified about Christ in relation to the Trinity. "according to the foreknowledge of God the Father, in the sanctification of the Spirit, for obedience to Jesus Christ and for sprinkling with his blood: May grace and peace be multiplied to you" (1 Peter 1:2).

Speaking of triple emphatics. There is one more subtle, yet powerfully important Trinitarian emphasis to mention. It brings comfort to the believer, and appropriately is still said to this day at the conclusion of worship—the Benediction. "The LORD bless you and keep you; the LORD make his face to shine upon you and be gracious to you; the LORD lift up his countenance upon you and give you peace" (Numbers 6:24–26).

The reiteration of "Lord" is Trinitarian in that it recurs three times, as well as to the contextual force of each specific reference. The Father blesses, the Son has a face which shines, and the Spirit indeed brings peace.

The man in the office of the priesthood is the mouthpiece of God reminding and bestowing this triple blessing

to God's people. The Trinitarian benediction bookends
the historical liturgical divine service which opens with
the invocation, "In the Name of the Father, and of the
Son, and of the Holy Spirit." The triune nature of God is
the beginning and end of the worship experience. These
invocations both reestablish and comfort the believer in
relation to God before reentering the world for the week,
where the devil lurks.

I would be remiss if I did not cite one other usage of
a triple emphatic, the number 666. This diabolical number referenced in the book of Revelation is a denotation
of the mark of the beast. The devil is less than God, and
imperfect. 666 symbolically implies the devil's desire to
be like the Triune God but ever underscoring his lack of
God's perfection. Satan is permanently short of God's
perfection, as six is forever short of the number seven.

QUESTIONS

1. Where has God woven the number three within His creation?

2. Why did Sarah laugh?

3. What is the sign of Jonah?

4. Why did Jesus set apart Peter, James, and John on several occasions?

5. Why did Jesus reinstate Peter three times?

6. What is the Trinitarian significance of the Benediction?

MEMORY

3	Three	Trinity	The Apostles Creed	The 3 Articles

THE NUMBER SEVEN

7

"Lucky number seven" is a classic line often cast about on the craps table of life. What is it about the number seven that makes it so *lucky* that people will literally bet on it? Seven naturally stands out with several unique qualities. It is the largest prime number from the most commonly used digits (1–10) and the only digit that has two syllables. The word *seven* even conveniently rhymes with *heaven* for the English speaker, which can subconsciously evoke a positive connotation. Seven indeed turns up frequently in many cultures around the globe, but it has nothing to do with luck.

God appears to use the number seven to underscore His work of perfection. God has woven it throughout all the cosmos, from sight and sound to space and time. There are seven colors in the rainbow, seven notes on the diatonic scale of music, seven continents, as well as the seven seas of antiquity. Classic medieval astrology recognized seven original *planets* observable with the naked eye (i.e., Moon, Mercury, Venus, Sun, Mars, Jupiter, and Saturn), which still correlate to the seven days in the week today. Seven is inescapably omnipresent, even to the eye of the unbeliever. We should not be surprised of its popularity in our culture today.

While seven is observable throughout much of creation, it is also repeatedly used throughout the Bible. Not only is seven considered perfect, it is linked to holiness. The seventh day of creation sets up the seventh day of the week as the Sabbath—the Lord's holy day of rest when everything was declared "Good." Accordingly, certain religious acts were performed seven times during specific worship rituals on the seventh day, or seventh month, or even the seventh year. The number seven innately speaks to God's divine standard.[10]

Because of this, the number seven can also help us remember the Lord's Prayer and each of its seven petitions. In this chapter, we will examine each of the seven petitions and explore several of the "seven" references throughout the Scriptures that reinforce the petitions themselves. Detecting all of this may require some special intelligence sleuthing though, so come along... *Agent 007.*

+++

The Lord's Prayer is powerful and perfect. Often times, people do not realize the entirety of what is spoken

---

10. St. Ambrose, *Letter to Horontianus.* "The number seven is good, but we do not explain it after the doctrine of Pythagoras and the other philosophers, but rather according to the manifestation and division of the grace of the Spirit; for the prophet Isaias has enumerated the principal gifts of the Holy Spirit as seven."

in this prayer. When we pray the Lord's Prayer, we are actually asking God seven specific requests.

The Lord's Prayer is what Jesus taught His disciples when they asked Him specifically to teach them how to pray. Christ's disciples were familiar with the prayers from the synagogues, but recognized how Jesus prayed in special ways, more profoundly than any other. They desired more. After all, John the Baptist had instructed his disciples to pray in a unique way. Similarly, Christ's disciples asked Him to teach them to pray.

Jesus said,

> "And when you pray, you must not be like the hypocrites. For they love to stand and pray in the synagogues and at the street corners, that they may be seen by others. Truly, I say to you, they have received their reward. But when you pray, go into your room and shut the door and pray to your Father who is in secret. And your Father who sees in secret will reward you. And when you pray, do not heap up empty phrases as the Gentiles do, for they think that they will be heard for their many words. Do not be like them, for your Father knows what you need before you ask him." (Matthew 6:5–8).

Once Jesus had finished correcting them on how *not* to pray, He spelled out for them how to pray. Jesus essentially taught them that there is a wrong way and a right way to pray, as there is a sinful way and a holy way to pray. Jesus continued to teach them to pray like this:

> "Our Father in heaven,
> hallowed be your name
> Your kingdom come, your will be done,
> on earth as it is in heaven.
> Give us this day our daily bread,
> and forgive us our debts, as we also have
> forgiven our debtors.
> And lead us not into temptation,
> but deliver us from evil" (Matthew
> 6:9–13).

As with any formal request, an address to the recipient is necessary for clarification. Accordingly, the Lord's Prayer begins with a simple introduction, making clear who the recipient is of our petitions to follow.

OUR FATHER, WHO ART IN HEAVEN

Even if alone, the immediate and all-inclusive usage of the word *our* comforts us in the knowledge that God has many beloved children and underscores the reassuring community aspect of the Church. We are not alone in this universe, not by a longshot.

HALLOWED BE THY NAME

God is holy and perfect, as is His name. God wants His name to be kept holy and perfect in the midst of His people. In this first request of seven, we ask God to help us keep His name holy.

There is a strong relationship with this first petition of the Lord's Prayer and the first table of the Ten Commandments; "You shall have no other gods before me, no graven images," "You shall not take the name of the Lord your God in vain," and "Remember the Sabbath and keep it holy."

It is natural to ponder, how indeed does one keep God's name holy as a sinner in the midst of sinners? Martin Luther laid out some helpful specifics of what this might look like in our daily lives: "We should fear and love God that we may not curse, swear, use witchcraft, lie, or deceive by His name, but call upon it in every trouble, pray, praise, and give thanks."[11]

Still we sin, we fail, so how can we keep His name holy, *perfectly*?

God shares His holiness and perfection with us through His word. He speaks to us into righteousness. Consider a Gospel approach when Jesus says, "Therefore, *be perfect*, as your heavenly father is perfect" (Matthew 5:48). Instead of trying to make ourselves perfect or attempting to keep His name holy among us for that matter, Christ makes us perfect as His gift to us and, therefore, allows His name to be holy among His people. The trick is for the perpetual sinner/saint to remain in contact with God's word, therein lies the friction with keeping this commandment.

---

11. Luther's *Small Catechism*, 2nd commandment, what does this mean?

Mankind was perfect at creation, but sin entered the equation. God sent His Son, Jesus, to pay for all the sins of the world by dying on the cross, and rising from the dead. Enter re-creation: resting in Christ. The Early Church Father Saint Augustine poignantly wrote, "Our hearts are restless, until we find our rest in God."[12]

When God perfectly created mankind, He did so with a specification—that mankind rests one day a week—a *seventh day's rest* to be specific. God even set a pattern leading by example and resting on the seventh day of the creation week.

Humanly speaking, if one keeps working in perpetuity, eventually sickness will result. We need a break, whether we want one or not. Our God says, "I will *make you* lie down in green pastures" (Psalm 23). Resting on one designated day of the seven-day workweek is healthy, needed, and innately aids in our request of God to help keep His name hallow.

God is the source of holiness, His Spirit gives us holiness, sanctifies and makes us holy. God provides what He requires of His people, to keep His name holy. Sunday worship (an echoing call to a seventh day's rest) is often referred to as the Divine Service. We are not praising and serving God in that time so much as God is *divinely serving* us.

Jesus says, "The Sabbath was made for man, not man for the Sabbath" (Mark 2:27). Christ comes as the true Sabbath, not to be served, but to serve. This truism further reveals who Christ is when He says "Come unto me,

---

12. Saint Augustine's *Confessions* (Lib 1, 1–2, 2.5, 5:CSEL 33, 1–5).

all who are weary laden, I will give you rest" (Matthew 11:28).

As an added bonus, in Christ, every day is a day of rest. Rest from all our afflictions can constantly be found in Christ's forgiveness, freedom, and grace. God is our hiding place and our refuge as the psalmist frequently declares (Psalm 119).

Luther concluded on this matter in his Small Catechism:

> "When the Word of God is taught in its truth and purity, and when we as the children of God also lead a holy life according to the word of God, that God's name be hallowed among us. Moreover, we also ask that God preserve us when anyone teaches contrary to God's Word."

God makes us holy and perfect by his Word. This is never more poignantly clear than when we are mindful of His seventh day's rest, a gift allowing us to keep His name hallowed among us.

+++

THY KINGDOM COME

Is the word *kingdom* a noun or a verb? Yes. When the word *kingdom* is translated from the original biblical Greek language into English, it is written as a noun. Consequently, when we pray "Thy kingdom come," we tend to seek a physical coming of Christ's kingdom and accordingly, scour the Bible for evidence of that location and power. However, the original Greek language accentuates the verbal base of the noun—the *activity* of a king. A king reigns, and Christ reigns with His grace and glory.

Pontius Pilate summoned Jesus before him and asked:

> "Are you the king of the Jews?" Jesus responded, "My kingdom is not of this world. If my kingdom were of this world, my servants would have been fighting, that I might not be delivered over to the Jews. But my kingdom is not from the world" (John 18:36).

When we pray, "Thy kingdom come," we pray not only for the arrival of Christ's kingdom on the Last Day, but also for our perfect and divine King of Kings, Jesus the Christ, to reign in and over our hearts, individually in the here and now.

This reign is of a spiritual realm. Eventually when Christ returns, there will be a new heavens and earth. We will once again experience His reign in an everlasting physical realm, as Adam and Eve once did. The number seven offers a bit of foreshadowing set up, as well as an eventual payoff concerning these realms, when Christ entered His glory.

Originally, God had created a perfect kingdom. The first seven words in the Hebrew Bible translate into English as, "In the beginning God created the heavens and the earth" (Genesis 1:1). Once paradise became lost, however, God's kingdom in creation became tarnished and sin-stained. Adam and Eve were no longer able to walk and talk in the presence of God in a perfect and holy physical kingdom. God foreknowingly and immediately went about the redemptive work of reestablishing a way for His people to physically be in His presence again, and not merely in a spiritual sense.

In Exodus, God continued building off His seven-day creation pattern, aiming towards a new creation. When the instructions for the tabernacle were specified to Moses on Mount Sinai, there were seven speeches God gave to Moses about designing the tabernacle. In the tabernacle God would dwell in a physical holy place in the midst of His people. An elaborate seven-day ordination process would be specified for priests. And God's seventh speech to Moses perfectly culminated with a teaching about the Sabbath and seventh day worship.

God's physical kingdom would only be an outline in this worship context, leading to something fuller and greater. All worship sacrifices were hollow compared to the fulfilling and ultimate sacrifice of Christ, when He entered His glory.

Flash forward to the New Testament. The mother of the Zebedee sons (James and John) approached Jesus with a vague request of Christ's kingdom of power.

> "Say that these two sons of mine are to sit, one at your right hand and one at your left, in your kingdom." Jesus eventually answers with, "...to sit at my right hand and at my left is not mine to grant, but it is for those for whom it has been prepared by my Father" (Matthew 20).

She would painfully understand none-too-soon.

When Jesus died for the sins of the world, He entered into His kingdom in glory, (with a crucified thief to His right and to His left). An observant Roman centurion declared, "Truly this was the son of God!" The Gospel writer then records this tender footnote in history:

> "There were also many women there, looking on from a distance, who had followed Jesus from Galilee, ministering to him, among whom were Mary Magdalene and Mary the mother of James and Joseph and the *mother of the sons of Zebedee*" (Matthew 27:54).

Presumably Mother Zebedee came to understand the broader magnitude of her earlier question.

Relevantly, Christ entered His kingdom (or reign) of glory upon the cross uttering seven different statements. Christ's famous last seven words from the cross further emphasize and fulfill the perfect nature of His atoning sacrifice. What does it mean when we pray, "Thy kingdom come?" Luther fittingly writes, "The kingdom of God comes by itself even without our prayer, but we pray in this petition that it may come to us also."

Saint Paul helps us understand this on an individual basis all the more. "He has delivered us from the domain of darkness and transferred us to the kingdom of his beloved Son" (Colossians 1:13).

How is this accomplished, might we ask? When our heavenly Father gives us His Holy Spirit, so that by His grace we believe His holy Word and lead a godly life here in time and there in eternity.

+++

THY WILL BE DONE ON EARTH AS IT IS IN HEAVEN

God's will flows freely and effortlessly in heaven where everything is pure, holy, and perfect. As for His will effortlessly flowing through us on earth, it is often met with resistance from the sinner. God's Word in the Scriptures rarely says what we *want* it to say. While His will certainly comforts and renews life to the sinner, more often than not it will afflict the all-too-comfortable sinner. In this situation we end up negotiating, bargaining, and glossing over sin. We try to impose *our* will, rather than God's.

When we pray this petition, we ask of God that He disrupt any influence that would guide us against His will, up to and including Satan, the worldly culture, and our own *better* judgment. We also continue to ask in this request that God deliver everything according to His promises.

God does allow mankind to experience free will, yet only over the things which God permits. Ironically, the one thing that could possibly save man, man cannot will himself toward—salvific faith in Christ. If we have willed against God, we deserve all the condemnation, yet if we enjoy salvation, God willing, Christ receives all the credit.

One major example in the Old Testament when God's will came from heaven to earth was in the form of the high holy day of Yom Kippur—the Day of Atonement. God desired for mankind to have a way to become clean and holy again. The best efforts of the will of man would never suffice. God exposed the Israelites unwillingness, yet prepared a way for them to be spared and brought into His will. The number seven would appear in connection with a ram slain for their atonement. This sacrificial event prefigured the Messiah, the Lamb of God, and His coming atoning sacrifice for all the world.

God declares a very specific time of the year for Yom Kippur. Here we have not merely a seventh day, but a specific day within the seventh *month,* according to the Hebrew calendar, set apart to reinforce His perfection.

Moses provides a detailed glimpse into the vast rituals of the sacred Day of Atonement.

> "And it shall be a statute to you forever that in the seventh month, on the tenth day of the month, you shall afflict yourselves and shall do no work, either the native or the stranger who sojourns among you. For on this day shall atonement be made for you to cleanse you. You shall be clean before the Lord from all your sins" (Leviticus 16:29–30).

Additionally, the blood from animal sacrifices was to be sprinkled on the altar by the priest seven times. "And he shall sprinkle some of the blood on it with his finger seven times, and cleanse it and consecrate it from the uncleanness of the people of Israel" (Leviticus 16:19). The sprinkling of the blood seven times signified that God's people were restored perfectly holy again by the blood of the atoning sacrifice.

Doing God's will is not easy, to put it mildly. We must consider and think it through. God's will does not flow naturally through us in our state of sin. Our sinful nature within wants to fight it and live in our own wild delusional freedom.

Thankfully, Christ demonstrated the ordeal of obedience to God's will. Once again, Jesus shows us the way. Saint Luke offers an extremely revealing close-up on Jesus in His state of humiliation, as He prays in the Garden of Gethsemane. He knows the horrors that are about to happen to His body, for He will be the perfect atoning sacrifice. With that divine foreknowledge Jesus prays, "Father, if you are willing, remove this cup from me. Nevertheless, not my will, but yours, be done" (Luke 22:42).

We should not be unsettled by Jesus seemingly *waffling* about whether or not He willed to die for us. Rather we should be comforted knowing His mortal flesh did not willingly look toward suffering any more than our own might in the same situation. Jesus dying on the cross was just as much a physical concern to Him than it would be to anyone else. His divine nature did not remove Him one iota from the extreme agony of the situation. All the more we can have faithful confidence that Jesus is exactly who He claims to be, fully God, and fully man at the same time—a perfect atoning sacrifice for the sins of the world.

+++

GIVE US THIS DAY OUR DAILY BREAD

Many of these seven petitions we ask of God are about massive larger-than-life themes. This next request reminds us that our God even cares about our seemingly small and little concerns, like where our next meal will come from.

Chances are if a random stranger is asked how many animals were brought aboard Noah's ark in preparation for the flood, the answer would be "two by two." This answer, however, would only be *half* correct. Often people are surprised to discover that God also directed Noah to bring animals aboard the ark, *seven by seven.*

> "Then the Lord said to Noah, "Go into the ark, you and all your household, for I have seen that you are righteous before me in this generation. Take with you seven pairs of all clean animals, the male and his mate, and a pair of the animals that are not clean, the male and his mate, and seven pairs of the birds of the heavens also, male and female, to keep their offspring alive on the face of all the earth. For in seven days I will send rain on the earth forty days and forty nights, and every living thing that I have made I will blot out from the face of the ground." And Noah did all that the Lord had commanded him" (Genesis 7:1–5).

The unclean animals brought two by two are there for creaturely preservation during the flood. The clean animals, that is the animals Noah's family could eat and/or sacrifice, were brought on seven by seven. Even on the ominous voyage of the ark, God perfectly provided a way for His people's daily bread, right down to the details of the packing list.

Another time God used the number seven to perfectly preserve His people with necessary nutrition, was through Joseph's interpretation of Pharaoh's dreams. Genesis chapter forty-one details Pharaoh's dreams. Initially, seven fat cows came up out of the Nile River, only to be swallowed up by seven skinny cows moments later. Additionally, Pharaoh dreams of seven healthy sprouting heads of grain, only to be swallowed up by seven thin and scorched heads of grains soon after.

Pharaoh and his wisest men were perplexed, until Joseph was summoned, from wrongful imprisonment. Joseph was granted a divinely appointed opportunity to interpret the dreams, spare Egypt in the process, and ultimately save God's people—with daily bread.

Joseph illuminated that there would be seven years of plentiful harvest, followed by seven years of severe famine. A vindicated Joseph rises to second in command of Egypt and shrewdly conserves the plentiful years of harvest in storehouses for preparation of the coming years of famine. Eventually, his own family, the Israelite line, would be drawn to Joseph seeking, of all things, daily bread.

Luther draws out the fact that God provides daily bread to both the wicked and the righteous.

> "God gives daily bread indeed without our
> prayer, also to all the wicked; but we pray
> in this petition that He would lead us to

know it, and to receive our daily bread
with thanksgiving."[13]

God would continue to be mindful of making sure His
people had their daily provisions and regularly employed
the use of the number seven in doing so. In Leviticus 23,
the Hebrew calendar is described. Certain holy day fes-
tivals involved eating and the number seven. The Feast
of Unleavened Bread was to be eaten for seven days.
Passover also involved a meal and an emphasis on the
seventh day.

Not to be outdone, the Festival of First Fruits or First
Grains emphatically used the number seven. It was celebrated on the day after a forty-nine day period of seven
weeks—seven weeks of seven days. This culminating fiftieth day would then be referred to in the Greek language
as *Pentecost* in the New Testament, celebrating agricul-
ture, harvest, and produce.

Ultimately, Christ would declare, "I am the bread of
life; whoever comes to me shall not hunger, and whoever believes in me shall never thirst" (John 6:35). The
eternally sustaining daily bread found in Christ points to
hungering and thirsting no more. What could be more
perfect than that?

+++

FORGIVE US OUR TRESPASSES, AS WE FORGIVE THOSE
WHO TRESPASS AGAINST US

---

13. Luther's *Small Catechism*

This petition exhibits God's crafty cleverness on full display. For as we pray for forgiveness from Him, it implies we are already forgiving others constantly, *right*?

Luther once again describes it this way in the catechism,

> "We pray in this petition that our Father in heaven would not look upon our sins, nor on their account deny our prayer, for we are worthy of none of the things for which we pray, neither have we deserved them; but that He would grant them all to us by grace; for we daily sin much and indeed deserve nothing but punishment. So will we also heartily forgive, and readily do good to those who sin against us."

In a classic exchange, Peter asks Jesus what many are too afraid, but dying to ask.

> "Then Peter came up and said to him, 'Lord, how often will my brother sin against me, and I forgive him? As many as seven times?' Jesus said to him, 'I do not say to you seven times, but seventy-seven times'" (Matthew 18:21–22).

Peter's use of the number seven implies he is aware of the significance of perfection associated with it.[14]

---

14. Gibbs, *Matthew* p.934 "Luz, *Matthew* 2:465 suggests that Peter's suggestion 'is by no means trivial. Seven is the traditional number of perfection.'"

Therefore, does perfect forgiveness look like forgiving someone seven times? Jesus trumps Peter's postulation with an eternal equation. Jesus' answer is not a literal product of multiplication but signaling a greater everlasting significance.

In the Old Testament, one of the most emphatic usages of the number seven in conjunction with the forgiveness of debts is the year of Jubilee. Much like a great version of Pentecost, Leviticus 25 lays out that after seven sequences of seven years, forty-nine years in total, the fiftieth year would be declared the year of Jubilee. During this Jubilee celebration the land would get a full year of rest. All debts would be restored, anything owed would be forgiven, separated families would be united, and property lost would be repaid and reacquired.

The year of Jubilee was one massive theological reboot of the system that was the nation of Israel. Every seven sequences of seven years this would take place, pointing to the permanent eternal Jubilation—Jesus Christ.

Jesus actually references this in His own words when He read aloud in the Temple.

> "The Spirit of the Lord is upon me, because he has anointed me to proclaim good news to the poor. He has sent me to proclaim liberty to the captives and recovering of sight to the blind, to set at liberty those who are oppressed, to proclaim the year of the Lord's favor." And he rolled up the scroll and gave it back to the attendant

and sat down. And the eyes of all in the synagogue were fixed on him. And he began to say to them, "Today this Scripture has been fulfilled in your hearing" (Luke 4:18–21).

Perfectly eternal forgiveness of sin, now that is something to be jubilant about.

+++

LEAD US NOT INTO TEMPTATION

It seems peculiar that we would ask God not to lead us into temptation, as if He is the one potentially leading us into temptation. God does not tempt us, but we request of God that we be protected from temptation by evil forces and that we be given the strength to overcome them.

King David illuminated the truth when he wrote. *"Thy word is a lamp unto my feet, and a light unto my path"* (Psalm 119:105). The world is a dark place. We are beset by temptation all around us. When we walk in Christ, the Word of God, His truth lights our path.

When God taught Moses with instructions about building the tabernacle, He also gave instructions for the functional, yet adorning equipment inside. One of those furniture items was the golden lampstand, also known as the *Menorah*.

It was dark inside the tent-woven tabernacle. There were no windows. The light inside came from the golden lampstand. It is described with tree-like qualities. It has a

stem, branches, and cups of blossoms, calyxes, and flowers. It was made of pure gold, from Egypt, and had lamps
illuminating the Holy Place—*seven* lamps to be exact.

> "You shall make a lampstand of pure gold.
> The lampstand shall be made of hammered
> work: its base, its stem, its cups, its calyx-
> es, and its flowers shall be of one piece
> with it. And there shall be six branches go-
> ing out of its sides, three branches of the
> lampstand out of one side of it and three
> branches of the lampstand out of the oth-
> er side of it; three cups made like almond
> blossoms, each with calyx and flower,
> on one branch, and three cups made like
> almond blossoms, each with calyx and
> flower, on the other branch—so for the six
> branches going out of the lampstand. And
> on the lampstand itself there shall be four
> cups made like almond blossoms, with
> their calyxes and flowers, and a calyx of
> one piece with it under each pair of the six
> branches going out from the lampstand.
> Their calyxes and their branches shall be
> of one piece with it, the whole of it a sin-
> gle piece of hammered work of pure gold.
> You shall make seven lamps for it. And the
> lamps shall be set up so as to give light on
> the space in front of it. Its tongs and their
> trays shall be of pure gold. It shall be made,
> with all these utensils, out of a talent of
> pure gold. And see that you make them

after the pattern for them, which is being shown you on the mountain" (Exodus
25:31–40).

The golden lampstand looked much like a burning
glowing bush or tree, offering light to the world. This
would have been comforting to Moses, perhaps reminding him of the presence of God at the burning bush. It
can also bring comfort to the Christian, in that Christ, the
Light of the World, also hung on a tree, that we might be
saved.

The very night Jesus was betrayed, He taught His disciples at the Mount of Olives, "Watch and pray that you
may not enter into temptation, the spirit is willing, but
the flesh is weak" (Matthew 26:42). The more we pray,
and gaze upon the light of Christ's truth, the less we may
feel inclined to give in to temptation and the darkness of
sin.

Jesus also said, "I am the light of the world. Whoever
follows Me will never walk in the darkness, but will have
the light of life" (John 8:12). The outcome of walking in
the light of Christ is being in His church, eternally.

John's vision in the book of Revelation mentions the
golden lamp stand again, but it is not alone—there are
seven of them—and declares:

> "As for the mystery of the seven stars that
> you saw in my right hand, and the seven
> golden lampstands, the seven stars are
> the angels of the seven churches, and the

seven lampstands are the seven churches"
(Revelation 1:20).[15]

Seven golden lampstands, representing the seven churches. God's perfect number, signifying all believing saints who have been made perfect by the blood of Christ, the Light of the World.

+++

DELIVER US FROM EVIL

Luther comments:

> "We pray in this petition, as the sum of all, that our Father in heaven would deliver us from every evil of body and soul, property and honor, and finally, when our last hour has come, grant us a blessed end, and graciously take us from this vale of tears to Himself in heaven."[16]

---

15. Brighton, *Revelation*, p.62 "The complete and holy number seven not only indicates that the seven churches represent all the churches, but it also suggests that all churches and all Christians are under the grace, forgiveness, renewal, guidance, and motivation of God through the sevenfold presence of the Holy Spirit (the seven Spirits" in 1:4). *The seven churches then symbolize the entire church of Jesus Christ under the motivating influence of the Holy Spirit.*"

16. Luther's *Small Catechism*

If you don't want to take Luther's word for it exclusively, consider Job's. "He will deliver from you six troubles; in seven no evil shall touch you" (Job 5:19). Job knew a great deal as a suffering soul, in body, property and honor, as well as being delivered from Evil.

God delivers us from evil in physical as well as spiritual ways. When the nation of Israel, led by Joshua, was making its way into the Promised Land, a number of issues arose concerning the local inhabitants. Body, soul, property, and honor were at stake regarding enticing the Israelites with false gods, evil culture and warring against them. An attack on the nation of Israel was essentially an attack on God. Therefore, God perfectly prepared the way to the Promised Land for His people.

Jericho had been shut up inside and outside because of the powerful presence of the people of Israel. None went out, and none came in. And the LORD said to Joshua,

> "See, I have given Jericho into your hand, with its king and mighty men of valor. You shall march around the city, all the men of war going around the city once. Thus shall you do for six days. Seven priests shall bear seven trumpets of rams' horns before the ark. On the seventh day you shall march around the city seven times, and the priests shall blow the trumpets. And when they make a long blast with the ram's horn, when you hear the sound of the trumpet, then all the people shall shout with a great shout, and the wall of the city will fall down flat, and the people

shall go up, everyone straight before him" (Joshua 6:1–7).

God perfectly and emphatically delivered them from evil.

Another profound Old Testament example of protecting the body while foreshadowing a spiritual protection of evil is in the story of Naaman, and the number seven would again carry an important role.

The play by play goes as follows:

> Elisha sent a messenger to say to him, [Naaman] "Go, wash yourself seven times in the Jordan, and your flesh will be restored and you will be cleansed." But Naaman went away angry and said, "I thought that he would surely come out to me and stand and call on the name of the LORD his God, wave his hand over the spot and cure me of my leprosy. Are not Abana and Pharpar, the rivers of Damascus, better than all the waters of Israel? Couldn't I wash in them and be cleansed?" So he turned and went off in a rage. Naaman's servants went to him and said, "My father, if the prophet had told you to do some great thing, would you not have done it? How much more, then, when he tells you, 'Wash and be cleansed'!" So he went down and dipped himself in the Jordan seven times, as the man of God had told him, and

his flesh was restored and became clean
like that of a young boy (2 Kings 5:10–14).

Naaman's body did not symbolically get healed of
leprosy, but actually physically healed, and he received
a changed heart of faith in the process. So too, we are not
symbolically forgiven by God in the waters of baptism,
but actually forgiven, delivered from evil, perfectly and
eternally.

+++

FOR THINE IS THE KINGDOM, AND THE POWER, AND THE GLORY, FOR EVER AND EVER. AMEN!

Saint Paul writes to his beloved pupil, Timothy, "The
Lord will rescue me from every evil deed and bring me
safely into his heavenly kingdom. To him be the glory forever and ever. Amen." (2 Timothy 4:18).

Martin Luther triumphantly echoes this sentiment
in his conclusion to this part of his catechism when he
wrote, "That I should be certain that these petitions are
acceptable to our Father in heaven, and are heard by Him,
for He Himself has commanded us so to pray, and has
promised to hear us. Amen, Amen that is, Yea yea, it shall
be so."

We can perfectly rest in the justifying work of Christ
for us, for it is His kingdom, His power, His glory.

Jesus himself declares seven "I Am" statements, making perfectly clear to all His hearers that He is God, the

great "I Am" and His encompassing works cannot be missed:

"I Am the Good Shepherd."
"I Am the Bread of Life."
"I Am the Light of the World."
"I Am the Gate."
"I Am the Vine."
"I Am the Resurrection and the Life."
"I Am the Way and the Truth, and the Life, no one come to the Father, but through me."

Biblically speaking, when seven is referenced there is an understated perfection to the use of it. He is our hiding place. We can pray and rest in that peace of perfection anytime and anywhere. As perfect as seven is according to God's usage and purpose, the seventh day of rest has been waiting for its fulfillment, literally, since the dawn of time, and what better way for God to do that than with the number eight.

QUESTIONS

1. Where has God woven the number seven through-out His creation?

2. What is the "kingdom" of God?

3. How many times should we forgive someone?

4. Why did Noah bring aboard the ark some animals 2x2 and others 7x7?

5. What were some of the priestly duties performed on Yom Kippur?

6. What is the origin of the menorah?

7. When did the year of Jubilee take place?

MEMORY

3	Three	Trinity	The Apostles Creed	The 3 Articles
7	Seven	Perfection	The Lord's Prayer	The 7 Petitions

THE NUMBER EIGHT

8

The biblical use of the number eight and the phrase "on the eighth day" carries significant weight. When we see the number eight appear in Scripture, it whispers of a connection to so much more, namely the Genesis of a new creation, God's covenant to us, how God chooses and marks us, and ultimately our baptismal faith. The number eight consistently hints at and helps us remember all of these themes and promises as we will explore in this chapter.

Has anyone ever broken a promise they've made to you? "Promises, promises," we often say with a skeptical shake of the head. We've all experienced an empty promise; a candidate that didn't deliver, an appointment that wasn't kept, a product that didn't work. Even the best and dearest among us are sinners, and can break their word occasionally. Maybe your dad promised a fun vacation experience, but he failed. Maybe someone promised to love you "until death do you part," but didn't.

People, even with the best of intentions, break promises. We've learned this all too well. And sometimes we unfortunately have permanent visual reminders when someone broke a promise with us; a bodily scar when you were assured of safety, a child from a broken marriage, massive debt after betrayal. Having faith in others can be extremely challenging. All people sin, and consequences remain from a sinner's broken promises.

God's promises however cannot be broken. We can have faith in His promises. It can be difficult to trust God's Word when everything else we endure in this world seems contrary, but God's Word never returns void. Christ never breaks a promise, and Christ makes us a big promise in baptism. Through baptism God gives us a visual and physical reminder of His promising Word. Luther's catechism phrases it this way, "Baptism is not just plain water, but it is the water included in God's command and combined with God's Word." In the liquescent ceremony of baptism we know God means business. This is one of His covenants to His people, and surprisingly, the number eight can help us remember this wonderful truth.

Eight connects strongly to faith in general, and the covenant of baptism specifically. Moreover, the numerous times eight appears in the Scriptures, faith underscores baptism and covenants. Baptism relates to faith in that it is not our word of promise to God, but rather God's Word of promise to us. In this way, God makes a covenant with His people. It is His word of promise and it does not break.

God establishes a covenant with each and every individual when they are baptized in the name of the Father, and of the Son, and of the Holy Spirit. Water is applied to the person during the baptismal ceremony and God's word works through it. Saint Luke helps clarify this is not

as a mere symbolic spiritual event, but an actual convey-
ing of the forgiveness of sins during the process. "And
Peter said to them, 'Repent and be baptized every one
of you in the name of Jesus Christ for the forgiveness of
your sins, and you will receive the gift of the Holy Spirit'"
(Acts 2:38).

It is important to note that salvific faith (the faith by
which we are saved) is not something manufactured or
produced within the human heart as an act of mankind.
Faith is a gift from God to mankind, created and given
by Him. A question often asked regarding saving faith is:
Where does faith come from? Saint Paul provides us with
a tremendously sufficient answer, "Faith comes from
hearing the message and the message is heard through
the Word of Christ" (Romans 10:17). God's proclaimed
Word creates everything in the universe, our faith
included.

There is a creational undercurrent to faith.

> "Therefore if anyone is in Christ, he is a
> new creation. The old has passed away.
> Behold the new has come" (2 Corinthians
> 5:17).

When we receive the gift of faith we become a new
creation.

In the Genesis account of creation, God began creation on the first day. He worked on the first six days,
morning and evening, and began rest on the morning of
the seventh day. Evening is never mentioned as it is for all
of the previous six days. This lingering sense of waiting
for completion leaves the door open and the light on for

a deeply significant understanding—eighth day theology. Not until Christ fulfills that seventh day rest will it lead to a new day—an eighth day—a day of new creation, faith, and life everlasting.

To better understand the foreshadowing of eighth day theology, consider another clue God leaves in Genesis where the number eight is not specifically mentioned, yet evident in such a powerful way that the New Testament can't help but expound on it. This pertains to the precise number of people aboard Noah's ark, spared during the great flood.

Chapter seven of the actual Genesis account mentions:

> "Noah was six hundred years old when the flood of waters came upon the earth. And Noah and his sons and his wife and his sons' wives with him went into the ark to escape the waters of the flood" (Genesis 7:6–7).

Simple arithmetic leads us to the sum of eight people. Genesis earlier mentions by name, Noah and his three sons, Shem, Ham, and Japheth, and that each entered the ark with their respective wife. Eight total people saved, passing through the raging waters, while the rest of humanity on earth drowned.

The story of Noah's ark and the flood is primarily of historical significance, yet God also uses it in a secondary way. The flood also serves as a theological foreshadowing for the ultimate redemption we have in baptism. For it is in baptism God also saves His people while passing through water. As Noah's family of eight passed through certain death to a new *re-created* world and newness of life, so the sinner drowns in a baptismal flood while the forgiven saint emerges.

Saint Paul further illustrates the point:

> "Do you not know that all of us who have been baptized into Christ Jesus were baptized into his death? We were buried therefore with him by baptism into death, in order that, just as Christ was raised from the dead by the glory of the Father, we too might walk in newness of life. For if we have been united with him in a death like his, we shall certainly be united with him in a resurrection like his" (Romans 6:3–5).

This is an extension of God's covenant to Noah down to the present age. God clarifies this immediately after the flood "Then God said to Noah and to his sons with him, behold, I establish my covenant with you and your offspring after you'" (Genesis 9:8). Astonishingly, the word *covenant* just so happens to be mentioned eight times throughout the entirety of the flood narrative, Genesis 6:9 – 9:17. Take that for what you will.

If you suspect it is a bit of a stretch to connect all these concepts of faith, covenant, and baptism to eight people saved through the flood, press the pause button. Recall what Peter writes in the New Testament:

> "Because they formerly did not obey, when God's patience waited in the days of

Noah, while the ark was being prepared,
in which a few, that is, eight persons, were
brought safely through water. Baptism,
which corresponds to this, now saves you,
not as a removal of dirt from the body but
as an appeal to God for a good conscience,
through the resurrection of Jesus Christ"
(1 Peter 3:20–21).

The floodwaters through which those eight people
were spared through still helps us remember God's promise with us today. Every time the rain waters fall, our baptismal faith can be enlivened by God's visual covenant on
display in the rainbow:

"I have set My rainbow in the clouds, and
it will be a sign of the covenant between
Me and the earth. Whenever I form clouds
over the earth and the rainbow appears
in the clouds, I will remember My covenant between Me and you and all living
creatures: Never again will the waters become a flood to destroy all life" (Genesis
9:13–15).

Promises, promises, God's promises are forever. His
promises of death to life, promises of forgiveness of sin,
promises of the restoration of all things, of a new creation, and a life eternal. God would not be done with visual, physical reminders of his covenant promise for faith,
or of using the number eight. The next time the number
eight appears, God would use a knife.

+++

"Let's cut a deal!" You may have heard that a time or two when someone has offered you an opportunity. That idiom actually has a biblical history to it. It harkens back to God cutting a covenant with the patriarch of the faith, Abraham.

The Old Testament often provides examples of cutting a covenant between two parties. An animal was slaughtered, and literally cut in two. Passing through the space between the opposite divided pieces was considered sacred. Typically, the two parties involved in the covenant would not be of equal power. Leverage would be different, with one entity being more powerful than the other regarding land, money, skill, or the sort.

Spoiler alert: When God cuts a covenant, He is *always* the more powerful party. Abraham brought nothing to the table. And God was about to promise everything to Abraham. Much like Genesis chapter one, God continues to create something out of nothing. God made specific promises to him; land, to make him a great nation, that God would bless him, make his name great, that Abraham would be a blessing, that God would bless those who blessed him, and that all people on earth would be blessed through him.

Not just any cut would do for these seven covenant promises in one, however. God had something unique in mind, and a particular day when this special cut should be executed. Can you guess which number of days links that covenant promise to us, echoing through all generations?

"This is my covenant, which you shall keep, between me and you and your offspring after you: Every male among you shall be circumcised. You shall be circumcised in the flesh of your foreskins, and it shall be a sign of the covenant between me and you. He who is *eight days* old among you shall be circumcised. Every male throughout your generations, whether born in your house or bought with your money from any foreigner who is not of your offspring, both he who is born in your house and he who is bought with your money, shall surely be circumcised. So shall my covenant be in your flesh an everlasting covenant. Any uncircumcised male who is not circumcised in the flesh of his foreskin shall be cut off from his people; he has broken my covenant" (Genesis 17:10–14).

It was a promised covenant mark from God to Abraham. If you had that eighth day mark of circumcision, you were counted in God's number—you were considered His chosen people. God chose Abraham, and brought him into the faith, as He does with everyone.[17]

---

17. Plass, *What Luther Says*, p.50 "The precept of circumcision is to be noted for use against the raging of the Anabaptists. For they hold that Baptism must be repeated and that adults only should be baptized, because infants do not have the use of their intellect and where this is lacking there can be no faith. But tell me: Circumcision is of benefit, as we have said, only because of faith. Now, God has

Another time the number eight occurs reinforcing this calling by God is the anointing of King David. God had dismissed Saul, the first king of Israel, and sent the prophet, Samuel, to Jesse. God tells Samuel "I have chosen one of his sons to be king." In perhaps the first un-taped episode of *The Bachelor*—a royally awkward version at that—Jesse one by one parades his sons before Samuel, but none are revealed to Samuel as God's chosen one. Samuel takes it from here:

> "Jesse had seven of his sons pass before Samuel, but Samuel said to him, 'The Lord has not chosen these.' So he asked Jesse, 'Are these all the sons you have?' 'There is still the youngest... He is tending the sheep.' Samuel said, 'Send for him; we will not sit down until he arrives.' So he sent and had him brought in. He was ruddy, with a fine appearance and handsome features. Then the Lord said, 'Rise and anoint him; he is the one.' So Samuel took the horn of oil and anointed him in the presence of his brothers, and from that day on the Spirit of the Lord came upon David in power" (1 Samuel 16).

David is also soon verified to indeed be the eighth and youngest son of Jesse. David—the eighth son—tending sheep in Bethlehem of all places, subtly highlights God's

---

enjoined the circumcision of infants on the eighth day and has given a very strong promise that He will care for them and preserve them."

choosing, the navigation of the Messianic line, and ultimately a royal priesthood of all believers to come. God
had been methodically stringing the pearls of promise for
generations before and for many generations to come.

God chooses His people and gifts them with a trace-
able mark, back through the annals of history, uniting
with His very covenant promise to our forefather of the
faith, Abraham. Moses recorded this important specification for the benefit of all Israelite generations to follow.
"And on the eighth day the flesh of the boy's foreskin is
to be circumcised" (Leviticus 12:3).

Our Christian faith today is linked to Abraham's faith
via the covenant of circumcision on the eighth day. This
eighth day covenant promise of God's slices through time
and space, from Abraham's son Isaac all the way to the
foreskin of the forerunner of Christ himself: John the
Baptist.

> "Now the time came for Elizabeth to give
> birth, and she bore a son. And her neigh-
> bors and relatives heard that the Lord
> had shown great mercy to her, and they
> rejoiced with her. And on the eighth day
> they came to circumcise the child. And
> they would have called him Zechariah af-
> ter his father, but his mother answered,
> 'No; he shall be called John'" (Luke 1:59).

And so, it was only a matter of time, and in line with the
Israelite tradition, the prophecies of the coming Messiah,
and the ultimate fulfillment of all things, that Jesus also
would be circumcised. This is of much weightier impact

than many Christians realize. For it was on the tender eighth day after Jesus's birth, with shepherds still marveling, when Joseph and Mary first brought Him to the temple.

> "When the eight days until His circumcision had passed, He was named Jesus, the name the angel had given Him before He had been conceived. And when the time of purification according to the Law of Moses was complete, His parents brought Him to Jerusalem to present Him to the Lord (as it is written in the Law of the Lord: 'Every firstborn male shall be consecrated to the Lord')" (Luke 2:21–23).

It was on that eighth day that Jesus was cut for the first time, for the entire world. The God in Christ, the Word made flesh, was circumcised and in so doing fulfills the covenant.[18] God bleeds His own blood for humanity and becomes associated with the typical pain of mortal sinful flesh. The blood of Christ that first flowed during that covenant ceremony served as an indicator of more suffering to follow.

---

18. Just, *Luke* p.119 "At the moment when his blood is first shed he receives the name given to him by the angel, Jesus. It is likely that Luke's hearers know what Matthew has recorded, that this means, "He will save his people from their sins" (Mt 1:21, cf. Acts 4:12, where "name" and "salvation" are sewed together). Already on the eighth day of Jesus's life, his destiny of atonement is revealed in his name and his circumcision."

This brings us to a pivotal point from the Old Testament to the New Testament.

Christ is Israel reduced to one. He is the bridge between the two, which fulfills the one covenant and extends it forward to this day. Some might argue that the covenant of eight day circumcision is extinct in the Christian Church today. Actual physical circumcision may be done for aesthetics or hygiene purposes, but there is no religious or Christian significance, per se. Oh, really? Not so fast! We are still *cut* with an eighth day covenant, just not in the way we customarily think. Christ marks us in the waters of holy baptism.

+++

The sequel to Lewis Carrol's beloved book, *Alice's Adventure in Wonderland*, is *Through the Looking Glass*. Alice gazes at a large reflecting mirror and discovers she can see beyond it. To her surprise, she is able to enter through the mirror into the fantastical wonderland where everything is opposite. Upon leaving the house (where it had been a cold snowy night), she steps into a sunny spring garden bursting with flowers; black is white, up is down, and backwards is forward.

Looking glasses, mirrors, and even reflecting pools offer dual intrigue in that one sees the reflecting surface itself, as well as one's own reflection. The still waters of a baptismal font can serve us very much like our own little reflecting pool. Let us gaze in and see where it leads.

Many people may merely see one aspect of baptism, as a law we should obey. Jesus literally commands this in the Great Commission: "Go therefore and make disciples of all nations, baptizing them in the name of the Father and of the Son and of the Holy Spirit, teaching them to observe all that I have commanded you. And behold, I am with you always, to the end of the age" (Mathew 28:19–20).

Luther once said, "Baptism is not simple water only, but it is the water comprehended in God's command and connected with God's Word." At a glance, baptism can appear one-dimensional, a divine regulation one *must* perform and check off the list of faith requirements as a dutiful believer, much like circumcision in the Old Testament. Saint Paul warns against this pitfall when he wrote to fellow Christians in Philippi regarding the danger of justifying one's self with the Law of God's Word (as a Pharisee might emphasize). The very first qualifier he cites is the specific day on which he was circumcised.

> "If someone else thinks they have reasons to put confidence in the flesh, I have more: circumcised on the eighth day, of the people of Israel, of the tribe of Benjamin, a Hebrew of Hebrews; in regard to the law, a Pharisee; as for zeal, persecuting the church; as for righteousness based on the law, faultless" (Philippians 3:4–6).

The Law alone just doesn't "cut" it for a sinner to achieve and attain salvation. The good news is there is more to God's Word than just the mirror of the Law. It leads to a deeper spiritual realm, further into God's Word. When we have been washed in the waters of baptism, we have the gifted ability to enter that reflecting pool, as it were, and appreciate the Gospel. In Christian faith we continue to discover and explore God's covenant promise in baptism and our new reality in Christ.

We are able to gaze beyond the Law as we experience the forgiveness of the Gospel. Through baptismal waters we can see two realities. We recognize the death of our former self, the sinner within us that drowned in the water and, at the same time, we also see the reflection of our new creation, for we are linked to Christ's own resurrection.

Thanks to the Gospel of God's Word, our world is opposite of what we've formerly known exclusively through the Law: What's lost is found, sin is forgiven, time once finite is now infinite, and death is swallowed up in life eternal.

Eighth-day covenant theology of circumcision relates to our baptismal theology today, as Christ gifts our faith to us. Paul illuminates this relationship forever when he links the law of eighth-day circumcision theology to baptism.

> "In him also you were circumcised with a circumcision made without hands, by putting off the body of the flesh, by the circumcision of Christ, having been buried with him in baptism, in which you were also raised with him through faith in the powerful working of God, who raised him from the dead. And you, who were dead in your trespasses and the uncircumcision of your flesh, God made alive together with him, having forgiven us all our trespasses,

by canceling the record of debt that
stood against us with its legal demands.
This he set aside, nailing it to the cross"
(Colossians 2:11–14).

All the same promises God made through the eighth-day covenant of circumcision are extended to us in baptism and point to a larger fulfillment of God's initial promises to Abraham.

The Promised Land on earth, is now the Promised Land that is the New Heavens and the New Earth to be enjoyed for all of eternity upon Christ's return. The great nation of Israel becomes that much greater and bigger as Gentiles are grafted onto that same branch and the Christian Church is the New Israel. We are blessed, not by a cut, but by the mark of baptism. Abraham's name continues to be great as the vast majority of people on earth trace their faith lineage back to him, Christians in addition to Jews and even Muslims.

Abraham will be a blessing, and he continues to be, as we preach the entirety of God's Word in the Scriptures, the Law and Gospel, to guide, comfort, and bless those who have ears to hear. God promised, "I will bless those who bless you, curse those who curse you" (Genesis 12:3). Jesus later declares in the beatitudes. "Blessed are you when people insult you, persecute you, and falsely say all kinds of evil against you because of me. Rejoice and celebrate, because great is your reward in heaven; for in the same way they persecuted the prophets before you" (Matthew 5:11–12).

God also promised, "All people on earth will be blessed through Abraham." The seed of Abraham's line ultimately led to Jesus, and Jesus died and paid for the sins of the entire world. Talk about a global blessing for all people.

Not only was Christ circumcised, but He was also baptized. Christ, who is the Word, is also the intersect for these seemingly two covenants, which are in actuality one covenant, that we might continue to see the Gospel in baptism, and not merely as a ceremonial law. Paul precedes his connection of eighth-day circumcision with baptism with these cautioning words:

> "See to it that no one takes you captive by philosophy and empty deceit, according to human tradition, according to the elemental spirits of the world, and not according to Christ. For in him the whole fullness of deity dwells bodily, and you have been filled in him, who is the head of all rule and authority" (Colossians 2:8–10).

Jesus was baptized, not for the forgiveness of His own sin, as we are baptized. Jesus's baptism is the opposite mirror image of our baptism. He is present in the water we are baptized in; thereby Christ takes on filth, sin, and death. In our baptism, we take on cleanliness, holiness, and immortality. He becomes associated with us, as we become associated with God.

While we are no longer physically circumcised on the actual eighth day, we are indeed divinely marked in baptism, representative of the eighth-day covenant. Artistic evidence demonstrates many older baptismal fonts have a hexagonal base. The six sides are meant to represent the six days of creation. And often the top of a baptismal font will be an octagon. The eight sides serve as a subtle reminder of the endless waves of the eighth-day covenant theology we still have today, splashing us in baptismal faith.

In every baptism, God once again creates something out of nothing. The baptized is united with Christ's death and Easter resurrection. A new creation comes to life, a new eternal day for the individual, by Christ's promise. Luther puts it this way:

> "It works forgiveness of sins, rescues from death and the devil, and gives eternal salvation to all who believe this, as the words and promises of God declare." Those declaring words of God are, "Whoever believes and is baptized will be saved, but whoever does not believe will be condemned" (Mark 16:16).

Do you doubt this eighth-day cutting covenant of God's is connected to creational baptismal faith and resurrection? It's okay to doubt for a while. One of Christ's very own disciples did. Thomas doubted—for precisely eight days—until he came to faith, believed, and became an apostle.

+++

Easter. Sunday. Sunday is the first day of the week according to the Judaic numbering pattern. Saturday was and is considered the seventh day of the week dating back to Genesis chapter one. Saturday remains the holy day, the worship day, the Sabbath day of rest according to the Jewish religion. While many Jewish people today merely acknowledge their ethnic traits, a portion of Jewish people still devoutly believe their religion, having rejected Jesus as the true Christ, and still await the coming of the Messiah. Christians, recognizing Jesus as the actual Messiah, worship a Sabbath day's rest on a Sunday. It is the day Jesus rose from the dead and the bedrock of the Christian faith. Every Sunday is a mini-Easter celebration linked back to that first Easter Sunday when the good news of the resurrection of the dead burst out. Easter Sunday, the first day of the week, another way to say that is—the Eighth Day.

That Easter day, the first day of the week, Jesus rose, destroyed death forever, and first appeared to Mary Magdalene. Saint John says, "On the evening of that day, the first day of the week..." (John 20:19). Jesus appeared to His disciples inside a locked room. He shared peace with them, showed them His crucified wounds, breathed the Holy Spirit upon them, and discussed the forgiveness of sins. There is peace, there is joy, for Jesus is risen from the dead. Death no longer exists. That proclamation heard round the world means that *that* first Easter day is *the* day—a day that has no end!

Jesus also shared with His disciples that evening, "As the Father has sent me, even so I am sending you" (John 20:21). Jesus is sending His disciples to share the important message of faith: the Gospel good news of the forgiveness of sins, the resurrection of the body, and the life everlasting. Yet there is seemingly one glaring problem. Thomas is not present.

In what could only be perceived as the meanest, darkest humored practical joke ever, Thomas had to enduringly listened to the other ten disciples' claim that Jesus had risen from the dead. Thomas responded, "Unless I see in his hands the mark of the nails, and place my finger into the mark of the nails, and place my hand into his side, I will never believe" (John 20:25).

In one light, "Doubting Thomas" doubts the resurrection of Christ. Examined another way, Thomas doubts the *testimony* of the resurrection of Christ by His disciples. If Thomas of all people struggled believing the original disciples' avouchment of Christ's resurrection, how could *anyone* take their word for it? Herein lies the great challenge and a teachable lesson for all of Christ's disciples today. Disciples of the Christian faith will always preach to doubting inquisitive skeptical ears, like Thomas, until the last day, questions like: "Did Jesus really rise from the dead?", "Will I actually rise from the dead too?", and "How can this be true?"

The matter of faith is at the epicenter of the entire resurrection narrative. Jesus chooses an intriguing number of days for Thomas and the other disciples to sweat out the doubt. John the Evangelist continues:

> Eight days later, his disciples were inside again, and Thomas was with them. Although the doors were locked, Jesus came and stood among them and said, "Peace be with you." Then he said to Thomas, "Put your finger here, and see my hands; and put out your hand, and place it in my side. Do not disbelieve, but believe."

Thomas answered him, "My Lord and my God!" Jesus said to him, "Have you believed because you have seen me? Blessed are those who have not seen and yet have believed" (John 20:26–29).

God knew faith would clash with doubt in a sinful world. The creation of faith was vitally needed for the Israelites, for Thomas, and for us, as it is critical for worship and continued proclamation. A new era was beginning—the Christian Church.

+++

This was not the first time God used the number eight to subtly reinforce the beginning of a new worship era. In Leviticus, after painstakingly preparing the building of the tabernacle, and a full seven-day priestly ordination ceremony for Aaron and his sons, God begins the Genesis of Israel's worship with these words:

"On the eighth day Moses called Aaron and his sons and the elders of Israel, and he said to Aaron, "Take for yourself a bull calf for a sin offering and a ram for a burnt offering, both without blemish, and offer them before the LORD" (Leviticus 9:1–2).

Faith is essential and required for God's people in a sinful world. God has embedded that message of eighth day creation of faith throughout the Scriptures, right from the very beginning. As mentioned earlier, "In the beginning" God spoke His Word and everything came into existence in a perfect sinless world. Adam walked and talked with God. Faith was not needed in that God was present and evident. God began His rest, Adam and Eve fell into sin, and the world would never be the same. God would therefore need to create faith for man.

The first chapter of Genesis describes the completion of the first six days with the phrase "there was evening and there was morning" for all of the first six days, Sunday through Friday. Yet peculiarly on the seventh day, a Saturday—the Judaic Sabbath day—that phrase is not stated. Morning is mentioned, but not evening. God begins resting, and the reader is left in a bit of suspense. The seventh day of the Judaic Sabbath's rest is only completely fulfilled much much later when Christ himself *rests* in the tomb, which also just so happens to be specifically on the Saturday Sabbath day of that holy week.

Christ, who takes the place of all sinful mankind from the first Adam, becomes the *second Adam*. Christ died on a Friday, the sixth day of the week. He rests in the tomb on Saturday, the Judaic seventh day of the week—morning *and* evening—and rises on Easter Sunday, completing the seventh day, thereby beginning a new day, an everlasting eternal eighth day in Christ. The author of Hebrews says, "So then, there remains a Sabbath rest for the people of God, for whoever has entered God's rest has also rested from his works as God did from His" (Hebrews 4:9–10).

The Judaic Sabbath day of rest serves us today as a sign pointing to Jesus, who *is* our rest. "Come to me, all who labor and are heavy laden, and I will give you rest" (Matthew 11:28). Since Jesus has come as our Savior and Lord, God no longer requires us to observe the Sabbath day and other holy days of the Old Testament. Christians since ancient times henceforth have regarded Easter Sunday as the Lord's Day, a new day of rest, for Christ rose on a Sunday. Every Sunday thereafter is a perpetual celebration of that eternal resurrection day.

If seven is the natural created perfect order of things, eight is suggestive of something supernatural, that which is beyond the natural order of this world. Eight represents infinity, and life eternal. The Early Church Father Saint Augustine referenced the significance of the eighth day in his reply to Faustus the Manichaean:

> "[Christ] suffered voluntarily, and so could choose His own time for suffering and resurrection, He brought it about that His body rested from all its works on Sabbath in the tomb, and that His resurrection on the third day, which we call the Lord's Day, the day after the Sabbath, and therefore the eighth day, proved the circumcision of the eighth day to be also prophetical of Him."

Acts 20:7 and 1 Cor 16:2 both reference the early church gathering "on the first day of the week," Sunday. Every Sunday, the first day of the week is a day of rest in the Lord and points expectantly to the ultimate Eighth Day—the final return of Christ, as every Sunday is a mini-Easter resurrection celebration day, and thus a celebration of the Eighth Day. The living and the dead in Christ will rise by faith and dwell with Him forever in the New

Heavens and the new Earth. Each Sunday drives towards the fulfillment of the day that will have no end.

God creates our faith and gives it as a gift to us. We do not have to rely on our own strength to have faith, we need only rely on His Good Word to us. Christ created everything in the universe, our faith included.

Luther beautifully teaches in question and answer: "What does baptism give or profit? It works forgiveness of sins, delivers from death and the devil, and gives eternal salvation to all who believe this, as the words and promises of God declare."[19]

In many instances God uses the number eight in the Scriptures which aids us to remember God's promises to us, His covenant, our baptism, and faith.

---

19. Luther's small catechism.

QUESTIONS

1. How does circumcision connect to baptism?

2. What does "resting in the Lord" look like?

3. Is Sunday the new Sabbath Day?

4. What is eighth day theology?

5. How are there two testaments, but only one covenant?

6. How does God pack all of His promises to Abraham into our baptism?

7. How can our baptism help us have faith in God's covenant to us?

8. What benefits does God give us in baptism?

MEMORY

3	Three	Trinity	The Apostles Creed	The 3 Articles
7	Seven	Perfection	The Lord's Prayer	The 7 Petitions
8	Eight	Promise	Baptism	8th Day Creation

THE NUMBER TEN

10

"You complete me." God teaches true completeness only comes from Him, despite what the venerable prophet, *Jerry Maguire*, may have said. God reveals to us in His word that we are incomplete because of our sin, and only He can make us complete again. The number ten is no more evidently found in the Scriptures than in the Ten Commandments, commonly referred to as His Decalogue and/ or the Law. It is difficult not to connect the thematic concept of completion and the number ten to the Ten Commandments.[20] The Law, and consequently God's judgment upon mankind, exposes our incompleteness when measured against it. This chapter will explore how God uses the number ten in the Bible which reinforces the concept of completion, particularly in the uses of the Law.

---

20. Petersen, *Fusion: Numbers* p.57 "To say there are Ten Commandments is to say the Law is complete. It covers every aspect of our lives."

The Ten Commandments make it painfully obvious that we are incomplete. Quite simply, no one measures up to God's standard with any level of significance. Christ alone measured up. He fulfilled the Law completely, and completes us, through the process of His passion. The number ten helps us remember the completeness of God's Law and how we fail to measure up to the standard of the Ten Commandments.

The Ten Commandments of the Lord as stated in Exodus 20:3–17 are:

> "You shall have no other gods before me. You shall not make for yourself a carved image, or any likeness of anything that is in heaven above, or that is in the earth beneath, or that is in the water under the earth. You shall not bow down to them or serve them, for I the Lord your God am a jealous God, visiting the iniquity of the fathers on the children to the third and the fourth generation of those who hate me, but showing steadfast love to thousands of those who love me and keep my commandments. You shall not take the name of the Lord your God in vain, for the Lord will not hold him guiltless who takes his name in vain. Remember the Sabbath day, to keep it holy. Six days you shall labor, and do all your work, but the seventh day is a Sabbath to the Lord your God. On it you shall not do any work, you, or your son, or your daughter, your male servant,

or your female servant, or your livestock, or the sojourner who is within your gates. For in six days the Lord made heaven and earth, the sea, and all that is in them, and rested on the seventh day. Therefore the Lord blessed the Sabbath day and made it holy. Honor your father and your mother, that your days may be long in the land that the Lord your God is giving you. You shall not murder. You shall not commit adultery. You shall not steal. You shall not bear false witness against your neighbor. You shall not covet your neighbor's house; you shall not covet your neighbor's wife, or his male servant, or his female servant, or his ox, or his donkey, or anything that is your neighbor's."

A minor controversy within Christendom over the last few centuries is that God's top ten list is not *specifically* numbered in the Bible. They are referred to as being the Ten Commandments (or ten words) and fully listed in two places (Exodus and Leviticus). Yet, in both instances they are written in unbroken text, without use of punctuation or numbers, as emphasized in their listing above. This leaves some slight wiggle room for interpretation.

The peccadillo of contention is whether or not "having graven images" should be included as part of the first commandment, essentially describing what it means to "have no other gods." The counterpoint: Should having no graven images be considered its own separate commandment?

Two main seeds of thought have grown apart from each other. Essentially, one branch consists of Judaism, the Eastern Orthodox, and many protestant churches today. This group of believers is in agreement with the Church Father Origen. They concur that having no graven images is a distinct commandment, and roll the concluding commandments of coveting together as one final commandment.

The second branch stems from the Church Father Saint Augustine, consisting primarily of the Roman Catholics, Lutherans, and a few other protestant churches. This group interprets "having no graven images" as part of the first commandment and towards the end makes a distinction between coveting living things from coveting material objects.

Augustine feared the forbidding of graven images would be misapplied by the iconoclast movement (destroying icons) and much of the beautiful early Christian art would be lost in its wake. By including "having no graven images" as part of the first commandment, and emphasizing a distinction with coveting, thankfully much of Christendom's early art has been preserved.

Essentially, one group splits the first commandment, and the other splits the last. Regardless, Exodus 34:28 as well as Deuteronomy 4:13 and 10:4 all describe the list as the "ten words." Both sides agree there are only a total of Ten Commandments and agree with the body of the Decalogue in its entirety.

Another aspect of the Ten Commandments is its two tables: one's relationship with God, and one's relationship with neighbors. Luther explains, "God wants us to trust Him above all else, to love Him, and to love our

neighbor." Lutherans conveniently have an advantage re-
membering this by way of their numbering system. Our
already familiar numbers of three and seven separate
these two tables of the commandments. The first three
(trinity) fittingly have to do with one's relationship with
God, and the remaining group of seven (perfection) have
to do with keeping a right relationship with one's neighbor and, essentially, with God as well.

+++

"You're out of bounds!" It never feels good to hear
that. Often the Law of God's Word is oversimplified as
being *bad*, while the Gospel of God's Word is watered
down with a mere label of *good*. This assessment is neither fair nor accurate. God's Word is always completely
true, pure, holy, and good—including the Law. The Ten
Commandments serve us as if a loving father put up a
boundary to defend His children from harm. Boundaries,
fences, curbs, even commandments protect us. The more
we live within the bounds and adhere to the Law of God's
Word, the more our lives tend to hum along well.

The Ten Commandments communicate what true
righteousness is, and our responsibility to that end.
Luther says in the *Catechism*, "The Ten Commandments
are God's Law, His good and loving will for the lives and
well-being of all people." They are a good gift given to us,
for our own benefit and protection, right down to our ten
little fingers and ten little toes.

There is an old Sunday school song that goes like this:
"Be careful little hands what you do ... Be careful little feet
where you go ... " (not to mention what we see, hear, and

say). It is only when we break the Ten Commandments, and cross the boundary, when real problems become evident. The Ten Commandments instantly reveal our failure and haunt us as we repeatedly learn the hard way that we cannot completely fulfill them. Thus, the Law at one point is described as a curse, "Christ redeemed us from the curse of the Law..." (Galatians 3:13). We feel sinful and incomplete as our righteousness and responsibility begin to blur. The Law of God's Word can even kill us with deathly damning poignancy. "For the wages of sin is death" (Romans 6:23).

Our generation is not the first to learn the hard way of what it means to go outside the boundaries God has established or to experience the resulting absence of holiness. The first major instance when the number ten appears in the Bible, a lack of righteousness is at the heart of the matter. Abraham actually attempted to haggle with God in some type of backwards auctioneer negotiation over the number of righteous people that may potentially be found in the cities of Sodom and Gomorrah. Ultimately, if ten righteous people could be found both cities would be spared from destruction. Abraham hedged his bet as best he could on his nephew, Lot, and his family hanging in the balance.

Fifty? Forty-five? Do I hear thirty-five? Twenty-five? Twenty? Abraham closes in,"'Oh let not the Lord be angry, and I will speak again but this once. Suppose ten are found there?' He answered, 'For the sake of ten I will not destroy it'" (Genesis 18:32).

The Law of God's Word can't even find one righteous man in Sodom—let alone ten. Let that burn into your mind. Don't be fooled to think Lot and his daughters were righteous. Lot showed grief, and perhaps some embers of repentance, but they were far from righteous. Yet as is typical for God's *modus operandi*, He allowed a remnant to be spared from His wrathful judgment upon the two cities.

Much later Jesus would offer a clue as to how righteousness and responsibility are reconciled through repentance. In the greater context of un-repentance and judgment upon cities that reject Christ, Jesus concluded a speech with the line, "I tell you that it will be more tolerable on the day of judgment for the land of Sodom than for you" (Matthew 11:24).

Unfortunately, Sodom and Gomorrah would not be the last time God would use the completeness of the number ten to demonstrate His judgment. God also specifically chose to use ten plagues to finally convince Pharaoh to let His people, Israel, go from Egypt.

The complete list of the ten plagues are: water turning to blood, frogs, gnats, flies, diseased livestock, boils, hail, locusts, darkness, and the death of the firstborn son. To further highlight the unrighteousness of humanity, Pharaoh couldn't help himself and ordered his army to chase after Israel. Pharaoh's army drowned in the Red Sea, while the remnant of God's people was spared.

Even in the midst of the wrath that played out with the ten plagues, God would still foreshadow a possibility of hope for righteousness. The first plague (water turning to blood) alludes to Christ's first miracle at the wedding in Cana, where He turned water into wine. The last of the ten plagues (death of the firstborn son) points to the last miracle of Christ's earthly ministry, death of God's only son—for the sins of the world. God was all but done signaling about His law with the number ten. It was time to be specific. God was preparing to send His first text message to His people, on a tablet no less.

+++

Scoring a perfect "10" takes complete excellence. Ask any Olympic gymnast. It is exceedingly difficult to score a "10." In fact, it's virtually impossible for most. The judges have a very strict and detailed scoring system to measure the athletes. When someone does score a "10" at the Olympics the world hears about it. That's how rare it is.

"And he gave to Moses, when he had finished speaking with him on Mount Sinai, the two tablets of the testimony, tablets of stone, written with the finger of God" (Exodus 31:18).

Finally the rules were written down, God's Law literally inscribed in stone. The Ten Commandments were complete and given to Moses, for Israel, and ultimately for all of humanity. Let the measuring of righteousness begin...

It would not take long for sin and unrighteousness to be self-evident to all. No sooner did Moses come down from Mount Sinai to share the Ten Commandments with the Israelites, did he get an eyeful of a sight he could not unsee.

It was panic at the disco.

If Moses had been told beforehand what would happen, he might never have believed. Moses's own brother (and soon to be high priest), Aaron, caved to the pressures of the people, built a golden calf statue out of molten jewelry, leading to war-like singing and worship with *dancing*, suspiciously suggestive of sensual indecency, familiar in Egypt. The great sin of adultery parallels cheating on God via idolatry.

Needless to say, there were no perfect "10s" scored that day. Even Moses dashed the original tablets of stone on the ground, righteous indignation towards unrighteousness. God's Ten Commandments were broken, spiritually and physically. Like an unflattering mirror that doesn't reflect what we want to see, the law was smashed, along with its sad reflection staring back at them.

Who can live without sin? How can anyone possibly measure up? If one can live the perfect life and follow the Ten Commandments completely, there is everlasting life to be enjoyed. Scoring a perfect "10" on God's scale when He is the judge is not just rare, not just scarce—it's one of a kind.

"The next day Moses said to the people, "You have committed a great sin. Now I will go up to the LORD; perhaps I can make atonement for your sin" (Exodus 32:30). If only one righteous person could be found to fulfill the Ten Commandments, score a perfect "10" and complete them, it would change everything, for everyone, forever. The world would hear about it...

+++

The Israelites would have to wait a long time for the coming of the Messiah. Meanwhile, God continued to teach them through His Law, exposing their unrighteousness, yet preparing a way for a remnant of them to be spared from condemnation. And the number ten would appear in connection to a ram slain for their atonement,

prefiguring the Messiah, the Lamb of God, and his atoning sacrifice for all.

We observed earlier the perfection of the seventh
month in Leviticus 16:29–30, but another look reveals
the importance of the specific day in that seventh month.

> "And it shall be a statute to you forever
> that in the seventh month, on the tenth
> day of the month, you shall afflict your-
> selves and shall do no work, either the na-
> tive or the stranger who sojourns among
> you. For on this day shall atonement be
> made for you to cleanse you. You shall be
> clean before the Lord from all your sins"
> (Leviticus 16:29–30).

God declares a very specific day of the year for Yom
Kippur. Here we have a magnification of two numbers,
the seventh month reinforcing perfection, yet performed
on the tenth day, recognizing the Law. The divine specifics of these numbers on the particular day suggest God's
people are made perfectly holy again by the blood of the
atoning sacrifice, while the Law of God is kept complete.

The Law of God's Word is the guiding source of truth.
Only when it is broken, do consequences arise. Inversely,
when God's Law is observed, there is a healthy rhythm
and flow to life. God uses the number ten again in the
form of a tithe to establish a standard of practice for community living, and to insure this quality of life to His people as well as the continued proclamation of His word.

"Every tithe of the land, whether of the
seed of the land or of the fruit of the trees,
is the Lord's; it is holy to the Lord. If a
man wishes to redeem some of his tithe,
he shall add a fifth to it. And every tithe of
herds and flocks, every tenth animal of all
that pass under the herdsman's staff, shall
be holy to the Lord" (Leviticus 27:30–32).

The Levites were the priestly tribe of Israel. To ensure
they could take care of God's house and God's people, the
tithe was established. The tithe simultaneously served as
a gift to God and as a way of taking care of the caretak-
ers of God's people. Eventually, when plots were parceled
in the Holy Promised Land, all twelve tribes of Israel received an allotment of land, all except the priestly tribe of
Levi. When God's people gave one-tenth of their earthly
blessings, the tribe of Levi was served, so they could in
turn serve God's people. Simply be faithful in that, and
the Israelite nation would remain strong and intact.

+++

You had one job.
Obedience to the Law does not pair well with waiting,
evidently. Israel would falter and fail, while Jerusalem
would fall a divinely appointed three times, to the
Assyrians, the Babylonians, and eventually the Persians,
before a spared remnant would return to Israel.
The divinely inspired standard of ten would percolate
up even during exile as the Prophet Daniel shared during the Babylonian experience. King Nebuchadnezzar

interrogated Daniel and company, ultimately putting them in his service. Nebuchadnezzar had an interesting reason.

> "In every matter of wisdom and under-
> standing about which the king questioned
> them, he found them ten times better than
> all the magicians and enchanters in his
> whole kingdom" (Daniel 1:20).21

A spared remnant of God's people would eventually find their way back to the Promised Land, weakly waiting for the Messiah to ultimately arrive on the scene. The fulfiller of the Law did come, and Jesus unsurprisingly had something to say about waiting and preparedness in a certain parable where he made use of the number ten. "Then the kingdom of heaven will be like ten virgins who took their lamp and went to meet the bridegroom. Five of them were foolish, and five were wise" (Matthew 25:1–2).

---

21. Steinman, *Daniel* p.102 "Ten times [better] (1:20) is the first time in Daniel that we find the use of a number in a symbolic or metaphorical way. Such uses of numbers will become more prominent in the visions later in the book. This is one example that refutes the dispensational rule that all numbers in prophecy must be taken literally. Certainly, 'ten times' does not represent a quantifiable measure of the Judeans' abilities relative to the other trainees. Instead, it signifies the surpassing nature of their skill and points the reader once again to God's control over the events even in Nebuchadnezzar's government. As later chapters will affirm, all the kingdoms of this world are subservient to God's kingdom."

Half the maidens were foolish in that they were not prepared with their oil lamps for the return of the bridegroom. When the moment of truth arrived, the foolish virgins had gone scrambling for supplies and missed the open door. They were not welcomed through the door (nor recognized) after the celebration began. The remaining half of the maidens who were prepared, entered through the door with excited anticipation. Familiar themes of obedience and complete faithfulness arise out of this story of ten. Some were doomed, but a portion was spared and saved.

The meaning underneath the parable of the ten virgins is that Jesus will ultimately return on the last day. Be ready, be faithful, and keep the light of Christ shining until then. An aspect of keeping watchful is mindful obedience to the Ten Commandments. You have one job, be diligent in the faith, for "no one knows the day or hour" (Mark 13:32) of Christ's return. If one is ill-prepared for Christ's return, it is an epic fail, bounced from the eternal banquet forever. Don't be a foolish virgin!

+++

The Ten Commandments of God bear a weight of expectation upon us. Jesus again reiterates this in another lesson where He employs the use of the number ten.

Christ shares another parable, this time of the ten minas.

> "A nobleman went into a far country to receive for himself a kingdom and then return. Calling ten of his servants, he gave

> them ten minas, and said to them, 'Engage
> in business until I come.' But his citizens
> hated him and sent a delegation after him,
> saying, 'We do not want this man to reign
> over us'" (Luke 19:12–14).

The burden of the law is unmistakable. Sinful mankind innately does not want to be reigned over by someone else's imposing rules, even (and perhaps especially) when it is God's Ten Commandments. Nevertheless, when they are observed and honored, life can be good. One might say even rewarding and full of blessings.

> "When he returned, having received the
> kingdom, he ordered these servants to
> whom he had given the money to be called
> to him, that he might know what they had
> gained by doing business. The first came
> before him, saying, 'Lord, your mina has
> made ten minas more.' And he said to
> him, 'Well done, good servant! Because
> you have been faithful in a very little, you
> shall have authority over ten cities'" (Luke
> 19:15–17).

The others produce less and receive proportionately less, but remain in the master's favor. Sadly, there is one who ignores the master's great expectation of the ten minas. He condemns the wicked servant. This judgment is indicative of those who shirk God's Law and speaks of eternal condemnation. There is zero leniency regarding God's Ten Commandments. No one but Christ alone can follow the Law of God completely and fulfill it. But don't take my word for it.

> "Do not think that I have come to abolish the Law or the Prophets, I have not come to abolish them but to fulfill them. For truly I say to you, until heaven and earth pass away, not an iota, not a dot, will pass from the Law until all is accomplished. Therefore whoever relaxes one of the least of these commandments and teaches others to do the same will be called least in the kingdom of heaven, but whoever does them and teaches them will be called great in the kingdom of heaven. For I tell you, unless your righteousness exceeds that of the scribes and Pharisees, you will never enter the kingdom of heaven." (Matthew 5:17–20).

Those who recognize and respect God's Law with any level of effort and repentance are spared and blessed beyond measure because of Christ's redemptive grace. Yet, those who dismiss and reject it entirely are doomed in condemnation, one might even say lost, save they repent.

+++

Have you ever lost something important? You may not have realized how intact and complete you were beforehand. Losing something precious can bring upon an aching sense of incompleteness. Jesus shares yet one more parable utilizing the number ten.

> "What woman, having ten silver coins, if she loses one coin, does not light a lamp and sweep the house and seek diligently until she finds it? And when she has found it, she calls together her friends and neighbors, saying, 'Rejoice with me, for I have found the coin that I had lost.' Just so, I tell you, there is joy before the angels of God over one sinner who repents" (Luke 15:8–10).

In the time of Jesus, it was a special custom for a woman to have ten silver coins woven into her bridal headdress. A Jewish girl would have literally scrimped and saved for such a headdress for her wedding day. Each coin was of great monetary and emotional value.[22] Losing one would be a huge deal and carry a strong sense of incompletion, not unlike losing a wedding band the night before the big wedding day in our culture.

The only good thing about losing something is the complete relief and joy when that something is found. Matthew, the evangelist, tucks this parable of the ten coins right in the middle of the parables of the lost sheep

---

22. Just, *Luke* CPH p585 "This is the only place in the NT where 'Drachma' occurs. A drachma is a Greek coin, equivalent to a Roman Denarius, estimated to be worth about a day's wage. Ten drachmas would be the life savings of a family, enough to see them through a period when no work could be found."

and the prodigal son to further emphasize the point. We are that precious something Jesus seeks after, the lost remnant to be spared. Jesus can relate with us searching for a lost precious something. We are lost in sin when the Ten Commandments are applied to us. We have been weighed, we have been measured, and we have been found incomplete.

While lost and incomplete, we tend to look for other things to complete us, and sin in the process. When we can't find what we are looking for, we settle for less in an attempt to fill the void in our life.

Instead of seeking a worship service to restore us, we settle for worldly entertainment. In place of seeking forgiveness from God via repentance, we make excuses in our attempt to justify ourselves. Rather than seek the wisdom of Christ's Word, we listen to the endless vapid sound bites of man, which still leaves us feeling incomplete. Only when we repent and receive forgiveness from God for our sin that we are once again found, restored, and completed. God invites us to celebrate with Him.

"'Rejoice with me, for I have found the coin that I had lost.' Just so, I tell you, there is joy before the angels of God over one sinner who repents" (Luke 15:9–10). And I imagine a fair bit of singing, too.

+++

"Be careful little hands what you do... Be careful little feet where you go..." as the song continues on. While that feels divinely threatening, the actual second half of each verse says, "There's a Father up above, and He's looking down in love, so be careful..." The Ten Commandments serve and protect us for our own cautionary good. In this way, God does indeed look down in love and care after us with the purity of His guiding word. Even after we break His word, God searches after us.

God always seeks a spared remnant from His judgment through atonement. Intriguingly, God inscribed His Ten Commandments with the use of His finger. There is only one other instance in all of Scripture where God writes specifically *with His finger*. Jesus does so once when He writes with His finger in the dirt. The onlookers held stones ready to pummel a woman caught in adultery.

While the Bible doesn't explicitly record what Jesus wrote, it is quite plausible to suppose it was the Ten Commandments. What else could Jesus write in that situation, that would convict everyone of their own sins, and prompt them to drop their stones and walk away? "Let him who has no sin cast the first stone" (John 8:7). No one remained but the fulfiller of the Law, Jesus himself, who did not condemn her. "Go, and sin no more" He concluded. Ironically, Christ was the only one who had no sin—and eventually He would be the first to cast a stone—the one blocking the empty tomb on Easter morning.

Christ heals us spiritually of our sin forever. He even heals us physically, at times temporarily on earth, and moreover, eternally with completely restored and resurrected bodies.

One last major story about Jesus where the number ten shows up is the healing of the ten lepers. This story is not a parable but an actual historical episode in Christ's ministry.

"And as he entered a village, he was met by
ten lepers, who stood at a distance and lift-
ed up their voices, saying, "Jesus, Master,
have mercy on us." When he saw them he
said to them, "Go and show yourselves to
the priests" (Luke 17:12–14).

They cry out to Jesus with more than desperation.
Jesus heals all ten lepers as He sends them to show themselves to the priest, not realizing they had just been in the
presence of the High Priest, Jesus.

All ten were healed, but only one of the ten (a tithe of
lepers) returns to say thank you. It further illustrates God
died for all, rose for all, and in so doing completed and
fulfilled the Law. He seeks after us, heals all, forgives the
sin of the world. And He does relish when we recognize,
repent, and receive His good works and say, "Thank you."

QUESTIONS

1. How are the Ten Commandments divided into two sections?

2. Why do some denominations number the commandments differently?

3. Who can "complete" the Law of God?

4. As Christ is the Alpha and Omega, how does He "work" through the ten plagues?

5. Why, possibly, would Jesus have written the Law with His finger in the dirt?

MEMORY

3	Three	Trinity	The Apostles Creed	The 3 Articles
7	Seven	Perfection	The Lord's Prayer	The 7 Petitions
8	Eight	Promise	Baptism	8th Day Creation
10	Ten	Completion	The Decalogue	10 Commandments

THE NUMBER TWELVE

12

One of the most iconic images of the Renaissance is Leonardo DaVinci's *The Last Supper*. It is an entrancing scene of Jesus breaking bread with His twelve disciples, on the very night He was betrayed. The painting is appropriately located in the refectory (dining hall) of a convent in Milan, Italy. The word *refectory* is derived from its Latin roots, which literally means "to remake or restore."

The act of eating nourishes and sustains the body. Christ is fully aware of the physical requirements of the human body. He connects with His people through ordinary bread and wine in more ways than one. While they break bread together, Christ also harnessed those elements sacramentally in order to spiritually restore His people until His final return. In the bread and wine of Holy Communion, Christ is both the giver and the gift.

This chapter will examine God's usage of the number twelve and consider how it can help us appreciate the institution of Holy Communion, as well as its role and purpose in the Christian Church. The number twelve is often used as representative of God's people; as the nation of

Israel in the Old Testament, the New Israel of the Church in the New Testament, but ultimately symbolic of all God's chosen people throughout all of time.

To start we must begin with the original Dirty Dozen, the twelve sons of Jacob. How dirty were they? The twelve sons are first mentioned in the context of this grim detail: "It came about while Israel was dwelling in that land, that Reuben went and lay with Bilhah, his father's concubine, and Israel heard of it. Now there were twelve sons of Jacob" (Genesis 35:22).

It is noteworthy that the father of the twelve sons is Jacob, which in Hebrew means *deceiver*. The twelve apples that fell from Jacob's deceiving tree didn't roll far. Jacob, however, eventually was redeemed by God, and given a new name. In a divine wrestling match, Jacob wrestled with the angel of the Lord, (the preincarnate Christ) who permitted Himself to be overcome. In reality, God allowed Jacob to be victorious, emblematic of Christ laying down His life for His people to "win" salvation.

God changed the name of the deceiver, *Jacob*, and gave him a name of redemption, *Israel*. "Your name shall no longer be called Jacob, but Israel, for you have striven with God and with men, and have prevailed" (Genesis 32:28). Similarly, Christ takes sinners and gives them His name of grace as Christians. God had a long game plan in mind of bringing that to fulfillment, and it began with the low-hanging fruit of Israel's twelve sons. "The sons of Leah: Reuben (Jacob's firstborn), Simeon, Levi, Judah, Issachar, and Zebulun. [24]The sons of Rachel: Joseph and Benjamin. The sons of Bilhah, Rachel's servant: Dan and Naphtali. The sons of Zilpah, Leah's servant: Gad and

Asher. These were the sons of Jacob who were born to him in Paddan-aram" (Genesis 35:23–26).

The original Dirty Dozen's rap sheet reads as such: murder, incest, usurpation, arrogance, conspiracy, and among other things, intent to commit fratricide. A who's who list of sinful treachery that would make even the most love-blind mother blush. If these were the first off-springs of Israel, and thus the line of the Messiah, much work was in order. God planned to feed them forgiveness, but first He would make them hunger for it. When God was through with them, the twelve sons would be starved for a better life for themselves as well as for their many descendants to come.

A literal famine in the land prompted all of Israel's twelve sons to end up in Egypt, save Joseph. He arrived much earlier as the reluctant recipient of a one-way ticket into slavery, courtesy of his jealous brothers. All were present except Benjamin, Joseph's lone full-blooded brother who shared the same mother, Rachel.

Joseph found himself imprisoned in Egypt, but not alone. The Lord was with him. Two other extremely sig-nificant individuals were also incarcerated: a baker and the cupbearer from Pharaoh's palace. The presence of the baker (of bread), and the cupbearer (of wine), should not be overlooked for their respective sacramental elements. Joseph's interaction with the two of them, via death and freedom, eventually paved the way for the twelve sons to dine together in peace. A fantasy that could only seem like a dream for Joseph, until God blessed him with a very unique ability.

"So the chief cupbearer told his dream to Joseph and said to him, 'In my dream there was a vine before me, and on the vine there were three branches. As soon as it budded, its blossoms shot forth, and the clusters ripened into grapes. Pharaoh's cup was in my hand, and I took the grapes and pressed them into Pharaoh's cup and placed the cup in Pharaoh's hand.' Then Joseph said to him, 'This is its interpretation: the three branches are three days. In three days Pharaoh will lift up your head and restore you to your office, and you shall place Pharaoh's cup in his hand as formerly, when you were his cupbearer. Only remember me, when it is well with you, and please do me the kindness to mention me to Pharaoh, and so get me out of this house. For I was indeed stolen out of the land of the Hebrews, and here also I have done nothing that they should put me into the pit.' When the chief baker saw that the interpretation was favorable, he said to Joseph, 'I also had a dream: there were three cake baskets on my head, and in the uppermost basket there were all sorts of baked food for Pharaoh, but the birds were eating it out of the basket on my head.' And Joseph answered and said, 'This is its interpretation: the three baskets are three days. In three days Pharaoh will lift up your head—from you!—and

hang you on a tree. And the birds will eat
the flesh from you'" (Genesis 40: 9–19).

Both of Joseph's interpretations rang true. The baker
was executed, and the cupbearer was exonerated and
put back in position. It took a literal nightmare scenario
for the cupbearer to finally—two years later—remember
Joseph to the Pharaoh. The Pharaoh had his own night-
terror dream questions plaguing him through his sleep.

Joseph was finally summoned via the cupbearer. He
interpreted Pharaoh's dreams with amazing understanding, and was freed. The Pharaoh, much more appreciative
than the cupbearer, promoted Joseph to the most powerful authority in the land, second only to the Pharaoh himself. Pharaoh would need Joseph. A severe famine was
coming after seven years of plenty, the same famine that
would prompt Joseph's brothers to seek food in Egypt.
Wise preparations and decisions needed to be made.

Joseph was blessed with foresight from God to store
up massive amounts of food during seven years of plenty,
ready to endure seven years of famine. It was only a matter of time for Joseph's brothers to show up grovelingly.
Joseph retained the upper hand as the brothers did not
recognize him.

> "'We are all sons of one man. We are hon-
> est men. Your servants have never been
> spies.' He said to them, 'No, it is the na-
> kedness of the land that you have come
> to see.' And they said, 'We, your servants,
> are twelve brothers, the sons of one man
> in the land of Canaan, and behold, the

> youngest is this day with our father, and
> one is no more.' But Joseph said to them,
> 'It is as I said to you. You are spies. By this
> you shall be tested: by the life of Pharaoh,
> you shall not go from this place unless your
> youngest brother comes here'" (Genesis
> 42:11–15).

Benjamin was not present (again) and the twelve
brothers were not complete. In a Machiavellian power
play, Joseph connivingly devised a way to have the brothers return home and retrieve Benjamin. After much stress
and family strife, which Joseph perhaps enjoyed in retali-
ation, Benjamin, the twelfth brother, finally made his entrance in Egypt.

> "When Joseph saw Benjamin with them,
> he said to the steward of his house, 'Bring
> the men into the house, and slaughter an
> animal and make ready, for the men are to
> dine with me at noon'" (Genesis 43:16).

So it was at 12 o'clock, all twelve sons of Israel shared
a meal, feasting and drinking freely together.

There is a Last Supper feel to this experience as the
twelve brothers dine together. Soon it would appear one
of them would betray the leader and Joseph was, for all
practical purposes, about to return from the dead in the
eyes of his brothers. Repentance and forgiveness were on
the horizon.

Before the brothers departed, Joseph hid his silver
cup, of all things, in Benjamin's sack. The ploy of planting

evidence of a heist that never happened worked perfectly. The eleven brothers headed back to their father, Jacob,
only to be stopped before their trip had barely begun.
Joseph's "missing" cup gave way to a rounding up of the
usual suspects. The brothers' bags were inspected with
plausible denial all the way down to Benjamin. Shocking
devastation followed when the cup was eventually pulled
from Benjamin's sack.

The brothers returned and pleaded with tormented
remorse. Joseph listened intently. The agonizing thought
of going home to their father without Benjamin, knowing
what they had done to Joseph, was too much to absorb for
all twelve brothers.

> "Then Joseph could not control himself
> before all those who stood by him. He
> cried, 'Make everyone go out from me.'
> So no one stayed with him when Joseph
> made himself known to his brothers. And
> he wept aloud, so that the Egyptians heard
> it, and the household of Pharaoh heard
> it. And Joseph said to his brothers, 'I am
> Joseph! Is my father still alive?' But his
> brothers could not answer him, for they
> were dismayed at his presence." (Genesis
> 45:1–3).

The twelve sons of Jacob were whole again. In the context of a cup, grain, famine, and feasts, the twelve brothers were restored by genuine sorrow and mercy. Joseph
could barely wait for Jacob to arrive. Their entire family

would rejoice, enjoying a luxurious life that God provided through Joseph for all their remaining days.

+++

The twelve sons of Jacob grew into the twelve tribes of Israel rather impressively over time. "The people of Israel were fruitful and increased greatly; they multiplied and grew exceedingly strong, so that the land was filled with them" (Exodus 1:7). So great were their numbers that a new Pharaoh, one who no longer remembered Joseph's contributions, became threatened. Through many dramatic twists and turns of God's providence, Moses was raised up. He was called to lead the twelve tribes of Israel back to the Promised Land of their forefathers, Abraham, Isaac, Jacob, and Joseph.

God used the ten plagues to prompt Pharaoh to let God's people go, an offer he couldn't refuse. The ten plagues were buttressed by the first (changing water into blood), and the last (death of the firstborn son). Appropriately, Christ's first miracle would be to change water into wine, and his last would be the death (and resurrection) of God's firstborn Son.

It is within this framework God chose to give instruction to His people to bake unleavened bread for their journey, and paint their doorways with the slaughtered blood of their finest lamb. The twelve tribes of Israel were prepped for their flight from Egypt as the angel of death passed over the land. The firstborn sons of all the homes in the land who had not marked their doorways with lamb's blood were slain, Pharaoh's included. The nation of Israel was free from slavery and departed under cover of darkness.

This sacred Passover meal would be observed and celebrated by the twelve tribes of Israel for an exceedingly long time. God had delivered them from bondage in Egypt. The meal meant a lot to God's people, until it meant more than they ever possibly imagined. Jesus would consecrate the Passover meal, fulfilling and enhancing its significance via his body and blood, through the bread and wine, for forgiving freedom from the bondage of sin. Bread and wine, body and blood, Holy Communion would become the doorway of God, delivering grace to His people, and for His people to enter an everlasting Promised Land.

> "Now as they were eating, Jesus took bread, and after blessing it broke it and gave it to the disciples, and said, 'Take, eat; this is my body.' And he took a cup, and when he had given thanks he gave it to them, saying, 'Drink of it, all of you, for this is my blood of the covenant, which is poured out for many for the forgiveness of sins'" (Matthew 26:26–28).

Faith in this sacred meal would prove to be vitally critical. Though, these deeper forthcoming concepts were far from the minds of the twelve tribes as they traversed the wilderness. They were still learning to have faith in God to provide for their hunger and thirst with ordinary food and drink, let alone spiritual.

After many painful lessons of hunger and thirst, God led them to the Promised Land. Before they could enter the land, a scouting report was needed. A reconnaissance mission was ordered to be sent out.

> "The Lord spoke to Moses, saying, "Send men to spy out the land of Canaan, which I am giving to the people of Israel. From each tribe of their fathers you shall send a man, every one a chief among them" (Number 13:1–2).

The twelve spies of Israel surveilled the land and, by request, brought back a remarkable item. They had been asked by Moses to see if the land was good or bad, who might currently dwell there, and to bring back some of the fruits of the land. The twelve spies returned with their report as well as the fruits. They brought figs and pomegranates, but the lead offering was the fruit of the vine—a cluster of grapes so large it was carried on a pole between two men.

The twelve spies described the Promised Land with food imagery—a "land flowing with milk and honey," yet the majority of the spies feared Israel could not overtake the local inhabitants. That lack of faith in God's promise quickly infused the twelve tribes, and Israel forsook God's gifted land to them.

Joshua, on point, finally addressed how good God's land for them was, and to have faith the Lord would deliver it to them. He then described the ease of taking over the oppositional people of the land in a most peculiar way:

> "Only do not rebel against the Lord. And
> do not fear the people of the land, for they
> are bread for us. Their protection is re-
> moved from them, and the Lord is with us;
> do not fear them" (Numbers 14:9).

The imagery of bread, and the fruit of the vine, proved
to be critical elements yet again, with the backdrop of
faith and God's deliverance to the Promised Land. The
twelve tribes of Israel would need a lot more time to sort
that out though. Four decades to be exact.

Eventually, God did lead the twelve tribes of Israel
to the Promised Land. Moses, representative of the Law
of God's Word, did not enter, however. He would only
gaze upon the Promised Land. It was Joshua, a prefigured
Yeshua, who would ultimately lead God's people through
the Jordan River and into the Promised Land. Naturally,
a ceremony was in order on such a momentous occasion.

> "When all the nation had finished passing
> over the Jordan, the Lord said to Joshua,
> "Take twelve men from the people, from
> each tribe a man, and command them,
> saying, 'Take twelve stones from here out
> of the midst of the Jordan, from the very
> place where the priests' feet stood firm-
> ly, and bring them over with you and lay
> them down in the place where you lodge
> tonight.' Then Joshua called the twelve
> men from the people of Israel, whom he
> had appointed, a man from each tribe. And
> Joshua said to them, 'Pass on before the

ark of the Lord your God into the midst of the Jordan, and take up each of you a stone upon his shoulder, according to the number of the tribes of the people of Israel, that this may be a sign among you. When your children ask in time to come, "What do those stones mean to you?" then you shall tell them that the waters of the Jordan were cut off before the ark of the covenant of the Lord. When it passed over the Jordan, the waters of the Jordan were cut off. So these stones shall be to the people of Israel a memorial forever'" (Joshua 4:1–7).

Twelve stones were incorporated as a monument for all of God's people to remember forever. Israel was permanently charged to not forget how the Lord brought His people to the Promised Land. In time, the nation of Israel seized the land, and established Jerusalem as the capital. They built a temple and adorned it with all of the furnishings God had previously directed them to build for the tabernacle. Among the ornamentals there were, specifically, twelve silver dishes, twelve silver bowls, and twelve golden pans to be used inside the temple, representative of each of the twelve tribes.

That isn't all they brought. The twelve tribes also brought with them all the religious customs God had taught them through Moses, Aaron, and Joshua. Another connection between bread and the inclusion of all God's people in the twelve tribes—a custom for the house of God first established by God in the wilderness.

"You shall take fine flour and bake twelve loaves from it; two tenths of an ephah shall be in each loaf. And you shall set them in two piles, six in a pile, on the table of pure gold before the Lord. And you shall put pure frankincense on each pile, that it may go with the bread as a memorial portion as a food offering to the Lord. Every Sabbath day Aaron shall arrange it before the Lord regularly; it is from the people of Israel as a covenant forever. And it shall be for Aaron and his sons, and they shall eat it in a holy place, since it is for him a most holy portion out of the Lord's food offerings, a perpetual due" (Leviticus 24:5).

The showbread of God, a constant present staple in the temple, was to be a permanent visual covenant, for all of God's people.

+++

God's people, in entirety, dwelled in the Holy Land. The twelve tribes had already been divided into four groups of three. In the wilderness the twelve tribes encamped around the tabernacle, always in the same groupings.

To the North were the tribes Dan, Asher, and Naphtali.
To the South, Gad, Simeon, and Reuben.
In the West lay Ephraim, Manasseh, and Benjamin.
And in the East; Judah, Issachar, and Zebulun.

When the tribes received their inheritance of twelve parcels of land, respectively, they followed a fairly similar pattern.

Two tribal names missing from the real estate deeds were Levi and Joseph. The absence of Levi owes to the fact that the tribe of Levi had been designated the priestly tribe. Their daily responsibilities involved the tabernacle, and later the temple. Their physical concerns were provided for off the tithes and offerings from all the other tribes.

In the absence of Joseph, two names are brought forth: Ephraim and Manasseh. They were the two sons of Joseph born to him in Egypt. Israel had the delight of laying his eyes on them when he journeyed to Egypt to be reunited with Joseph. On Israel's death bed, Israel passed down blessings to all his sons, and incorporated Ephraim and Manasseh into the family lineage as well. Joseph effectively became the firstborn as the older brothers, for one sinful reason or another, were passed over. Moreover, Joseph became doubly blessed as his blessing was spliced into his two sons, essentially making them co-firstborn by proxy.

A major factor to consider is the fact that Ephraim and Manasseh were not full-blooded Hebrews. They were Joseph's sons, but born to him from an Egyptian woman, and therefore a Gentile wife. The legitimizing of Joseph's two sons by Israel further magnifies God's original promise to Abraham, and points to the hopeful possibility of more Gentiles being grafted into the twelve tribes of God's people.

+++

Jesus finally arrived, and with great implication He specifically chose twelve disciples to follow Him.

> "In these days he went out to the mountain to pray, and all night he continued in prayer to God. And when day came, he called his disciples and chose from them twelve, whom he named apostles: Simon, whom he named Peter, and Andrew his brother, and James and John, and Philip, and Bartholomew, and Matthew, and Thomas, and James the son of Alphaeus, and Simon who was called the Zealot, and Judas the son of James, and Judas Iscariot, who became a traitor" (Luke 6:12–16).

A new era had begun, yet God's usage of the number twelve was still utilized to convey the entirety of God's people.[23] In the Old Testament, twelve represented all of the nation of Israel. In the New Testament, twelve also became representative of all of God's people in the church—the New Israel.

The twelve disciples followed Jesus and, in time, would become the foundation of the church. First, however, Jesus needed to instruct them. As pointed out earlier, the first miracle Jesus performed was in front of His twelve disciples. He changed water into wine at a certain wedding in Cana. That got their attention pretty well.

---

23. Roehrs and Franzmann, *Concordia Self-Study Commentary*, p.47 "The appointment and sending of the twelve is the declaration of His mercy to the whole of Israel, (12 tribes)."

Another miraculous teaching lesson, Jesus integrated the number twelve in connection with a meal for hungry masses. With a crowd gathered of 5,000 men (not to mention women and children), Jesus nourished the crowd by a miracle. He collected five loaves of bread and two fish, blessed the provisions, and directed the twelve disciples to pass and share. Everyone ate plenty and there were even leftovers. Jesus performed a similar miracle to 4,000 people in attendance.

On one level, it was amazing what Jesus accomplished for the people. On a second level, there was more going on than met the eye. It was not the act of the miracles that was so exclusively important, but also the meaning behind them. We need not speculate, Jesus laid it out for His disciples:

> "When they went across the lake, the disciples forgot to take bread. 'Be careful,' Jesus said to them. 'Be on your guard against the yeast of the Pharisees and Sadducees.' They discussed this among themselves and said, 'It is because we didn't bring any bread.' Aware of their discussion, Jesus asked, 'You of little faith, why are you talking among yourselves about having no bread? Do you still not understand? Don't you remember the five loaves for the five thousand, and how many basketfuls you gathered? Or the seven loaves for the four thousand, and how many basketfuls you gathered? How is it you don't understand that I was not talking to you about bread?

> But be on your guard against the yeast of
> the Pharisees and Sadducees'" (Matthew
> 16:5).

Jesus called attention specifically to the *number* of baskets of leftover food at each of the miraculous meals. Jesus speaks as if the specific numbers of extra baskets should mean something.[24] We have examined the number seven in depth. It is perfection, woven throughout all seven continents of creation. Twelve is the church of God's people, and there will be a great need for future feedings of God's Word. While there is the yeast of bad teaching to be wary of, it is as if to say the Church is called to share God's Word with the world.

Christ is the Bread of Life. He is the miraculous meal to nourish all people. He is to be shared to all ends of the earth.

> "I am the bread of life. Your ancestors
> ate the manna in the wilderness, yet they
> died. But here is the bread that comes
> down from heaven, which anyone may
> eat and not die. I am the living bread that
> came down from heaven. Whoever eats
> this bread will live forever. This bread is

24. Gibbs, *Matthew*, p.752 "The amount of leftover fragments—twelve baskets—has suggested to some an "Israel/people of God" accent (see Hagner, Matthew 2:418). This also seems likely to me. It is the Messiah of Israel who thus provides for the lost sheep of Israel's house. The twelve baskets may also be a reminder of an anticipation of the twelve apostles present in 26:20."

my flesh, which I will give for the life of
the world." Then the Jews began to argue
sharply among themselves, "How can this
man give us his flesh to eat?" Jesus said to
them, 'Very truly I tell you, unless you eat
the flesh of the Son of Man and drink his
blood, you have no life in you. Whoever
eats my flesh and drinks my blood has
eternal life, and I will raise them up at the
last day. For my flesh is real food and my
blood is real drink. Whoever eats my flesh
and drinks my blood remains in me, and I
in them'" (John 6:48–56).

Christ would die, rise, and ascend with a promise to
return. Until then, Christ, the Word, the Bread of Life
Himself is to be shared. Future feedings will be needed for
all of God's people until the Last Day. The number twelve
would remain evidence of an all-inclusive representation
of God's people. It was essential. Just ask Mathias.

After Jesus had charged the disciples with the Great
Commission and ascended into heaven, the disciples observed they were not intact. They were but eleven, for
Judas had committed suicide. A twelfth disciple was
necessary.[25]

---

25. Roehrs and Franzmann, *Concordia Self-Study Commentary* CPH
ACTS, P107 "When Jesus appointed the twelve apostles (Lk 6:13), He
was offering His Messianic grace and laying His Messianic claim to
the twelve tribes, to ALL Israel. After Jesus intercession for the people
who crucified Him (Lk 23:34), that offer and claim is to be state anew.
Therefore Judas *must* be replaced (22), God wills that all Israel be

"For," said Peter, "it is written in the Book of Psalms: 'May his place be deserted; let there be no one to dwell in it,' and, 'May another take his place of leadership.' Therefore it is necessary to choose one of the men who have been with us the whole time the Lord Jesus was living among us, beginning from John's baptism to the time when Jesus was taken up from us. For one of these must become a witness with us of his resurrection" (Acts 1:20–22).

The number twelve will remain symbolically significant for the Church, the New Israel, all the way to Christ's return on the Last Day, and into eternity.

"And Jesus said to them, "Truly I say to you, that you who have followed Me, in the regeneration when the Son of Man will sit on His glorious throne, you also shall sit upon twelve thrones, judging the twelve tribes of Israel" (Matthew 19:28).

+++

John, the last of the twelve apostles to live, wrote a vision of the Last Day. In the book of Revelation, John describes the end of this world, and the beginning of a new world, creation restored. He used a most unusual number

confronted with the crucified and risen Christ and so be offered His forgiveness anew."

to convey all of God's people that come out of the Great Tribulation to enjoy eternal righteousness with God:

> "After this I saw four angels standing at the four corners of the earth, holding back the four winds of the earth to prevent any wind from blowing on the land or on the sea or on any tree. Then I saw another angel coming up from the east, having the seal of the living God. He called out in a loud voice to the four angels who had been given power to harm the land and the sea: Do not harm the land or the sea or the trees until we put a seal on the foreheads of the servants of our God.' Then I heard the number of those who were sealed: 144,000 from all the tribes of Israel" (Revelation 7:1–4).

Each tribe is listed accordingly, with 12,000 from each totaling 144,000. 144,000 is a biblical number in strong relationship to 12. John's Revelation is the only instance it is used, and in a context of symbolic language. Are there literally only 144,000 people going to heaven? Certainly not! Why this specific number? It would appear once again that God likes to use certain numbers to convey meaning.[26] $12 \times 12 \times 10^3$ (144,000) is a calculatedly poetic way to describe the entirety of God's people of the

---

26. Brighton, *Revelation*, p.62 "In Revelation the number twelve and its multiples twenty-four and 144,000 represent the church of God as church."

Old Testament, multiplied by God's people in the New Testament, multiplied by Trinitarian completeness.

John saw merciful comfort in the Revelation vision, the fulfillment of Christ's promise, He saw the Church triumphant:

> "After this I looked, and behold, a great multitude that no one could number, from every nation, from all tribes and peoples and languages, standing before the throne and before the Lamb, clothed in white robes, with palm branches in their hands" (Revelation 7:9).

It is a very vivid and accurate Gospel snapshot of how all of God's people will dwell in the promise of His grace forever.

The Church has been grafted into God's Dirty Dozen, but made clean by Christ crucified. We all have our issues. We all have this difficult walk of life set before us. We all have been forgiven and then some, yet as Christians we all have been sealed by God. We know we have this great picture of the truth of the Church triumphant, but we are not there yet.

While we continue to live and get dirty with sin, God has a way to clean and sustain us, feeding us forgiveness. His body, His blood, in, with, and under the bread and the wine. God's people continue to be fed by that forgiving meal until the Last Day. A few verses later in the same context, John provides this morsel of detail: *"They shall hunger no more, neither thirst anymore; the sun shall not strike them, nor any scorching heat"* (Revelation 7:16).

The number twelve, God's people, Israel fulfilled as the Church of Christ, and nourished by His miracle of Holy Communion—until life everlasting.

QUESTIONS

1. Were the twelve sons of Jacob all from the same mother?

2. What was the significance of the two people Joseph met in prison?

3. How did Ephraim and Manasseh become part of "the twelve" tribes?

4. Why didn't the tribe of Levi receive a parcel of land in the Promised Land?

5. Why was Mathias added to the twelve Apostles?

6. Was Judas actually present when Jesus instituted Holy Communion?

MEMORY

3	Three	Trinity	The Apostles Creed	The 3 Articles
7	Seven	Perfection	The Lord's Prayer	The 7 Petitions
8	Eight	Promise	Baptism	8th Day Creation
10	Ten	Completion	The Decalogue	10 Commandments
12	Twelve	The Church	Holy Communion	12 Tribes/ Apostles

THE NUMBER FORTY

40

We have examined the thematic biblical usage of the numbers 3, 7, 8, 10, and 12. What does it all add up to? Fascinatingly, the sum of the previous five numbers is 40. Forty is a reoccurring number in the Bible that often signifies the coupling of testing and hope. The mathematical relationship with forty as the sum of the other numbers is a textbook reminder that can actually serve us. It is almost a suggestive hint: When we live our faith reconciling these doctrines, it leads to a constant vacillation between testing and hope, for the sinner/saint that is every Christian.

This chapter will focus on the number forty's relationship with testing and hope, some of the prominent places it is used in the Scriptures, and how that can help us remember confession and absolution.

Martin Luther once wrote:

> "For God delays action out of grace, in our best interest, that our faith may become strong and great and He may give all the more abundantly what He has promised.

For it is the nature of God to come slowly, but to come without fail. Just so, He also punishes slowly but punishes terribly. He grants one time and opportunity enough to come to one's senses and to improve. For this reason the elect must wait and be patient for the sake of the wicked, that the honor of God, that He is long-suffering and does not promptly punish, may stand. Therefore, the patience of the godly and the wickedness of the ungodly last so long. But God comes in due time in order to recompense both richly."[27]

This concept is readily and intimately experienced through the process of repenting of sin and receiving forgiveness. It can at times be a meticulously slow and painful process for the individual to withstand.

Confession and absolution is typically referred to as "the Office of the Keys" in pastoral parlance. This phraseology comes from the pairing of two texts. In the first one Jesus says:

"I will give you the keys of the kingdom of heaven. Whatever you bind on earth will be bound in heaven, and whatever you loose on earth will be loosed in heaven" (Matthew 16:17).

---

27. Plass, *What Luther Says*, p.391.

In another text, post crucifixion and resurrection, Jesus greets His disciples and expounds on this concept when He says, "If you forgive anyone his sins, they are forgiven; if you withhold forgiveness from anyone, it is withheld" (John 20:23).

When one is unrepentant of sin, there is a *locking* of separation, and a closing off from God's forgiveness. Correspondingly, when one receives forgiveness from God, there is an *unlocking* and openness to God's forgiveness. The testing and wrestling through confessing one's own sin can be an exhausting struggle. Sinners are notoriously stubborn. However, after the fear and repenting of said sin passes, hope is immediately realized. Hearing the spoken words of forgiveness absolves the sinners from their sin and leads to grace, mercy, and peace.

Confession and absolution serves a bit like God's escape room of testing and hope, customized for each individual. When we are trapped in sin, the door to God's grace is closed and locked. Time ticks by, yet the only solution is for the door to be unlocked. We try to wiggle our way out. We convince ourselves, if we tinker and fidget enough, we just might find another passageway to freedom. Any path opposed to confessing sin seems preferable. The truth remains, there is only one way out.

Sin must be confessed. The vexed sinner tries to avoid it, gloss over it, justify it, and pretend, anything in order to escape God's judgment, but to no avail. The only hope for righteousness and freedom is through the door of Christ and the forgiveness of sin. Solomon poetically alludes to it this way "An evil man is trapped by his rebellious speech, but a righteous man escapes from trouble" (Proverbs 12:13).

The first major instance of the number forty in the Bible must have felt quite literally like the world's first actual escape room.

> "Then the Lord said to Noah, 'Go into the ark, you and all your household, for I have seen that you are righteous before me in this generation. Take with you seven pairs of all clean animals, the male and his mate, and a pair of the animals that are not clean, the male and his mate, and seven pairs of the birds of the heavens also, male and female, to keep their offspring alive on the face of all the earth. For in seven days I will send rain on the earth forty days and forty nights, and every living thing that I have made I will blot out from the face of the ground.' And Noah did all that the Lord had commanded him" (Genesis 7:1–5).

A lot of testing was tossed around those torrential waters for Noah and his family, but hope apparently does float. A new world and new life loomed for those aboard that special vessel. An eventual Promised Land of a renewed creation awaited them on the other side of the trial that was the initial forty-day flash flood.

+++

God foreshadows testing and hope towards a Promised Land, new life, and forgiveness repeatedly throughout the Scriptures, and the number forty is frequently used to call our attention to this promise. Hope is always centralized around the Gospel of Christ, testing on the other hand, is usually different for individuals in various ways.

Testing is a broad and general word. We appreciate knowing specifically what a test will entail. God allows many trials for His people to face; from fasting and taunting, or waiting and long-suffering, to exile and obedience, God leads His people to ultimate hope in Him. A hope God alone can give exclusively toward salvation and life everlasting. Unfortunately, mankind excels at putting false gods as obstacles in the way of God's promises.

This lesson was brutally drilled into God's people when Moses had to scale Mount Sinai and receive the Ten Commandments—*the second time*. We recall the first time after Moses had received them. He descended upon the Israelite community only to discover them partaking in worshipping the golden calf. Moses consequently shattered the tablets out of righteous indignation. Moses then reclimbed the mountain into the presence of Yahweh, no doubt full of a wide spectrum of emotions.

> "And the Lord said to Moses, 'Write these words, for in accordance with these words I have made a covenant with you and with Israel.' So he was there with the Lord forty days and forty nights. He neither ate bread nor drank water. And he wrote on the tablets the words of the covenant, the Ten Commandments" (Exodus 34:27–28).

Fasting is a popular testing method still used today in conjunction with the number forty, as observed during the liturgical season of Lent. Fasting is distinctive in that it has a way of fine-tuning faith toward hope. Moses fasted for forty days, addressing the issue of idolatry. He took the onus of the sins of the people upon himself, confessed as intermediary to God, and eventually secured absolving grace from God for the people. This particular episode of testing and hope led to the giving of God's Word of Law in written form. God's Law could not be perfectly upheld by any normal human. It would ultimately be fulfilled by God in Christ alone, on behalf of the people. Jesus took the onus of sin upon himself to secure grace for the world.

The pesky sin of idolatry is a chronic issue with God's people, but thankfully God is a God of do-overs and second chances. This would be both good news and bad news for the Israelites, or perhaps more precisely, bad news followed by good news in the form of more testing and hope.

+++

The exodus ensured the Israelites would no longer "walk like an Egyptian." They had traversed through the wildland and camped for a season at the base of Mount Sinai. They had been the benefactors of numerous incredible moments of divine assistance: The Passover and flight from slavery, the miraculous crossing of the Red Sea, the manna from heaven, the presence of Yahweh at Mount Sinai, and the building of the tabernacle. One would think it was obvious to all that God was with them. One would think.

The Israelites were on the verge of an assured permanent oasis from their travails. Twelve spies, one from each tribe, were sent in from the outer rim of the Promised Land to examine and gather intel for their imminent seizing of the land. The spies literally stared the Promised Land in the face for forty days, but doubt arose within them during this reconnaissance mission. They became unsure if they could actually take over the land for themselves. The issue at stake? Lack of faith.

> "At the end of forty days they returned from spying out the land. And they came to Moses and Aaron and to all the congregation of the people of Israel in the wilderness of Paran, at Kadesh. They brought back word to them and to all the congregation, and showed them the fruit of the land. And they told him, 'We came to the land to which you sent us. It flows with milk and honey, and this is its fruit. However, the people who dwell in the land are strong, and the cities are fortified and very large...'" (Numbers 13:25–28).

None of the other aforementioned miraculous escapades of Israel were easy, yet God delivered them victorious every time. Seizing the Promised Land, even with a vast and powerful community occupying it, would be putting their faith in action. God would deliver them once again and give them the gift of the Promised Land. By faith, this was as certain as any previous miraculous work of God they had witnessed.

Alas, the discord of doubt prevailed. Ten of the twelve spies dissented strongly. They did not believe they could actually succeed in seizing the promised holy land. Notably, Joshua and Caleb were *not* part of the naysaying company.

The faction of faithless spies grew louder, spreading false words and fear throughout the Israelite community. The majority of the Israelites regressed into a mob mentality and their shouts soon reached a fever pitch. They were literally ready to hurl stones at Moses, Aaron, Joshua, and Caleb, or anyone who ventured forth from the lineup in opposition to them. Perhaps the world's first cancel culture was on the scene.

Needless to say, God was less than thrilled.

> "And the Lord spoke to Moses and to Aaron, saying, 'How long shall this wicked congregation grumble against me? I have heard the grumblings of the people of Israel, which they grumble against me. Say to them, "As I live, declares the Lord, what you have said in my hearing I will do to you: your dead bodies shall fall in this wilderness, and of all your number, listed in the census from twenty years old and upward, who have grumbled against me, not one shall come into the land where I swore that I would make you dwell, except Caleb the son of Jephunneh and Joshua the son of Nun. But your little ones, who you said would become a prey, I will bring in, and they shall know the land that you have rejected. But as for you, your dead bodies shall fall in this wilderness. And your

children shall be shepherds in the wilderness forty years and shall suffer for your faithlessness, until the last of your dead bodies lies in the wilderness. According to the number of the days in which you spied out the land, forty days, a year for each day, you shall bear your iniquity forty years, and you shall know my displeasure." I, the Lord, have spoken...'" (Numbers 14:26–35).

Forty years of wandering in the wasteland, for forty days of wondering if God would truly be with them. That was the cost of speaking badly of what God had declared good. They would learn a new definition of testing and hope. The Promised Land would indeed come, in due time as God had assured, but to the next generation.

Joshua would eventually lead them to the Promised Land, pointing toward Jesus (Yeshua) ultimately leading God's people to *the* Promised Land of everlasting life, and to the New Heavens and New Earth. Before any of this though, many tests would come toward the Israelites in the wilderness during those forty years. Tests of obedience and patience, and perhaps even reflection of confession and absolution, with a hope to look forward in faith. To ponder the promises of God in relation to repentance. To wonder as they wandered.

They would have plenty of time to think about it. I'd like to tell you that that was the only time the Israelites had to endure forty years in order to learn a lesson from God.

I'd *like* to tell you that.

+++

Israel finally entered the Promised Land, but the sin of envy soon sprung up. The Israelites wanted a human king like all of their bordering nations. God was their King, but the people rebelled desiring a physical king. God instead chose to give them judges. Many prominent judges came and went, Gideon, Ehud, Deborah, but the Israelites were never truly satisfied, for they still desired to "keep up with the Joneses" and have their very own king, just like their many surrounding neighbors. Consequently, God used another forty years to remind them of His sovereignty. "And the people of Israel again did what was evil in the sight of the LORD, so the LORD gave them into the hand of the Philistines for forty years" (Judges 13:1).

Hope did indeed arrive after forty years in a most ominous way, prefiguring the eventual arrival of the Messiah. God sent an angel to a woman, barren and childless, with the news that she would conceive and bear a son. The birth of Samson was hope personified, and indeed pointed toward another angelic annunciation of a son to a young woman, who would too be born, rise, rule, and die to deliver God's people.

Samson was gifted with colossal strength by the Lord and became one of the judges of Israel. He would lead and save God's people from the Philistines, yet not before much testing and hope.

Samson, though titanic and powerful with the Lord, was not impervious to sin. He foolishly divulged his God-given secrets to his Philistine wife, Delilah. Sweet pillow-talk soon went sour. What happened next could only be described as the worst episode ever of *Real Housewives of Israel.* Delilah covertly ordered her native Philistines to shave off Samson's seven braids of hair—the Divinely-blessed source of his strength. Delilah was paid for her traitorous actions with pieces of silver. Samson awoke to discover the might of the Lord had left him, and was promptly bound, blinded, and forced into slave labor by the Philistines.

A Philistine celebration was in order after Samson had been sequestered. He was summoned to perform before the vile throng in their temple. Samson cunningly requested to be chained to two pillars holding up the structure of the building. With his strength zapped—locked out of God's blessing of strength upon him—Samson pleaded to God in prayer:

> "Then Samson prayed to the LORD, 'Sovereign LORD, remember me. Please, God, strengthen me just once more, and let me with one blow get revenge on the Philistines for my two eyes'" (Judges 16:28).

An early rudimentary form of confession to be sure, followed by an absolving outpouring of Godly strength upon him one final time.

> "Then Samson reached toward the two central pillars on which the temple stood. Bracing himself against them, his right hand on the one and his left hand on the other, Samson said, 'Let me die with the Philistines!' Then he pushed with all his

might, and down came the temple on the
rulers and all the people in it. Thus he
killed many more when he died than while
he lived" (Judges 16:29–30).

The next time the number forty would glaringly occur, it would be many generations later. Though the san-
dal would be on the other foot, for the seemingly mighty
one. A destined descendent of Israel *would* remember
God's forty-year lessons, that Israel should not be defied,
and the Lord, Yahweh, was indeed with His people.

+++

"Sticks and stones may break my bones, but words
will never hurt me," was probably not on the minds of
the Israelite army when Goliath taunted them. They still
ran and fled, like their fearful forefathers before them.
Though a measly little stone would soon enough inflict
its damage upon the giant Goliath.

Samuel the priest provides the dastardly details:

"And there came out from the camp of
the Philistines a champion named Goliath
of Gath, whose height was six cubits and
a span. He had a helmet of bronze on his
head, and he was armed with a coat of
mail, and the weight of the coat was five
thousand shekels of bronze. And he had
bronze armor on his legs, and a javelin
of bronze slung between his shoulders.
The shaft of his spear was like a weaver's

beam, and his spear's head weighed six hundred shekels of iron. And his shield-bearer went before him. He stood and shouted to the ranks of Israel, 'Why have you come out to draw up for battle? Am I not a Philistine, and are you not servants of Saul? Choose a man for yourselves, and let him come down to me. If he is able to fight with me and kill me, then we will be your servants. But if I prevail against him and kill him, then you shall be our servants and serve us.' And the Philistine said, 'I defy the ranks of Israel this day. Give me a man, that we may fight together.' When Saul and all Israel heard these words of the Philistine, they were dismayed and greatly afraid." (1 Samuel 17:4–11).

How long did the jeering juggernaut test Israel with his pejorative jabbing? "For forty days the Philistine came forward and took his stand, morning and evening" (1 Samuel 17:16). Being tested is never fun, and this was quite the torturous taunt.

David had apparently received the message that the armies of the living God should not be defied, that *and* the opportunity for fortune and glory. After David had talked with his brothers on the front line, of how King Saul would majestically honor the one who might slay Goliath, it was more than enough. It was a chance at legendary heroism every young boy dreams of, to go into the breach, solo, for all the credit.

King Saul looked upon young David, armed with only a slingshot. He deliberated between David's divinely inspired gusto, or his potentially magnificent delusion of grandeur. Eventually, David's bravery ruled the day as Saul said to him, "Go, and the LORD be with you!" The Lord indeed was. David opted out of Saul's size XXL armor and went to face his fate.

The shepherd boy, with stones still wet from the brook whence he pulled them, barked back at the behemoth,

> "You come to me with a sword and with a spear and with a javelin, but I come to you in the name of the Lord of hosts, the God of the armies of Israel, whom you have defied. This day the Lord will deliver you into my hand, and I will strike you down and cut off your head. And I will give the dead bodies of the host of the Philistines this day to the birds of the air and to the wild beasts of the earth, that all the earth may know that there is a God in Israel, and that all this assembly may know that the Lord saves not with sword and spear. For the battle is the Lord's, and he will give you into our hand" (1 Samuel 17:45–47).

Everything David spoke rang true after his first stone zinged into Goliath's brow. The Philistine army fled. The taunting of God's people came to an end. A new day had arrived, in the victory—through David—God had provided for them. The Israelites had front row seats to see hope spring when even one of God's people has faith that the Lord will be with them, in battle, or in life. If only they could remember it.

David would be no stranger to confession and absolution, as his Psalm writing would later reveal. God, however, would continue to teach His people that slaying one's foe is not the only way to get rid of them.

+++

Hating an enemy is never a simple problem to overcome. Another tender lesson God taught His people was that God forgives, even and most particularly when His people don't think certain others *should* be forgiven. Nonetheless, confession and divine absolution are God's arrangements to orchestrate.

Proclaiming grace to those we hate, and loving our enemies, is one tall order of a test. The prophet Jonah learned this the hard way. When God *voluntold* Jonah to head toward Nineveh, Jonah was less than thrilled, to say the least. He ran.

Running from God is not good. Anytime one does not obey the Word of God, it is considered sin. Jonah shirks God's call to go to Nineveh because it was the capital city of the Assyrians. They were a nasty people, with a different culture. They were regarded as the scum of the earth as far as the Israelites were concerned, including Jonah. Jonah believed they did not deserve to receive the grace of Yahweh.

Wrestling with sin that needs to be confessed can cause a sinking into despair. Jonah's depravity literally descends as the biblical narrative plays out. He goes *down* to Joppa, *down* into the inner part of the ship, he laid *down* to sleep, goes *down* into the waters of the raging seas, and *down* into the belly of the whale. All the while God's Word pursued him.

Only after Jonah finally repents and confesses his sin, does the whale vomit him *up* onto dry land. Yahweh has creative ways of humbling people. He reiterated to Jonah, that He is in fact a God of second chances, as He repeated his original request, "Arise, go to Nineveh, that great city, and call out against it the message that I tell you" (Jonah 3:2).

Jonah experienced a type of death when he went *down* unto Sheol, and rose again, very much emblematic of the process of the death and rebirth experience via repentance and forgiveness. The inner toil of confessing sin before God can seem like a death, due to the unknown nature that lurks on the other side of said confession. The recreative grace awaiting the sinner on the other side of penitence never fails to surprise. When God speaks "arise" out of the pit of despair, it is resurrection language. This is fitting for the newness of life and gospel absolution Jonah receives from God.

The reluctant prophet finally obeyed God "So Jonah arose and went to Nineveh, according to the word of the Lord. Now Nineveh was an exceedingly great city, three days' journey in breadth. Jonah began to go into the city, going a day's journey. And he called out, 'Yet forty days, and Nineveh shall be overthrown'" (Jonah 3:3–4).

The Ninevites were aptly given forty days to repent for their sins.[28] Though they did not appear to require that

---

28. Lessing, *Jonah* p.298 "Forty is a stock biblical number that couples testing and hope... ...the number forty works eschatologically: the

much time, or even the amount of time Jonah needed, to turn to the Lord. The immediate following verse reads: "And the people of Nineveh believed God. They called for a fast and put on sackcloth, from the greatest of them to the least of them" (Jonah 3:5).

God did exactly what Jonah had feared. He shared His love and forgiveness to detestable people. Because Jonah still loathed the Assyrians of Nineveh, he found the matter reprehensible, which says more about Jonah than the Ninevites.

> "But it displeased Jonah exceedingly, and he was angry. And he prayed to the LORD and said, "O LORD, is not this what I said when I was yet in my country? That is why I made haste to flee to Tarshish; for I knew that you are a gracious God and merciful, slow to anger and abounding in steadfast love, and relenting from disaster. Therefore now, O LORD, please take my life from me, for it is better for me to die than to live" (Jonah 4:1–3).

Jonah needed a minute.

Confession and absolution is a powerful concept to absorb, especially when it means loving an enemy. When

---

fortieth is the last day, when the goal arrives, which shapes the content of the preceding thirty-nine days (or years). Under the pressure of the last day, the preceding days become pregnant with a new beginning, and life begins in a new way."

people receive what they don't deserve, it can be a bit hard to swallow.

+++

Israel repeatedly struggled during their forty-day tests, and rarely held fast to their newfound teachings very long. God would bring them through, with hope culminating at the end each time, but like routine clockwork afterward they fell away. One instance, even Judah, the southern kingdom, a reduced portion of Israel, did not prove successful. Whereby God called the Prophet Ezekiel to lay on his side forty days, one for each of the forty years they sinned against God. If that sounds bad, consider the 390 days he was called to lay on his other side for the years of sins for the northern kingdom of Israel, prior to that!

If only one could fulfill this litany of misery and put an end to it.

Enter Jesus, and the New Testament. The prophecies of the Messiah have finally come true. Christ the Savior has arrived. Jesus was born and grew into adulthood without much pomp or circumstance. As a full grown man, He was ready to begin his work.

Jesus, freshly baptized to fulfill all righteousness by John the Baptist, headed into the wilderness. Jesus had a very specific forty-day fasting mission on His mind.[29] He

---

29. Gibbs, *Matthew*, p.194 "In much greater and contrasting measure, Jesus, God's Son, is led into the desert, and his personal fast of forty days and forty nights corresponds to Israel's forty years in the wilderness."

was preparing for the start of his earthly ministry. "And Jesus, full of the Holy Spirit, returned from the Jordan and was led by the Spirit in the wilderness for forty days, being tempted by the devil. And he ate nothing during those days. And when they were ended, he was hungry" (Matthew 4:1–2).

Jesus was inches from the goal line at the conclusion of the forty-day fast when the devil emerged with his temptations. The fact that there were three temptations perhaps subtly highlights the trinitarian quality of Christ's divine nature triumphing where sinful man had failed. Christ resolutely prevailed in each of the three temptations.

The devil's temptations had to do with hunger, idolatry, and most poignantly—testing the Lord. These were areas Israel had easily succumbed to earlier. Yet, Jesus emphatically answered each specific temptation with relevant Old Testament references where Israel had broken the Law.

> The devil said to him, "If you are the Son of God, command this stone to become bread." And Jesus answered him, "It is written, Man shall not live by bread alone'" (Matthew 4:3–4).

Soon after Israel's exodus from Egypt, they found themselves grumbling against God in the wilderness. They gripe aloud:

> "It is better to die than starve in the wilderness." Jesus certainly could use His power

to turn stones into bread. He would eventually demonstrate similarly at the miraculous feeding of the 5,000. However, there
Christ would do so to serve others. Here
Christ refused to serve Himself. "He hum-
bled you, and in your hunger He gave you
manna to eat, which neither you nor your
fathers had known, so that you might understand that man does not live on bread
alone, but on every word that comes from
the mouth of the LORD" (Deuteronomy
8:3).

The second temptation revolved around idolatry.

And the devil took him up and showed
him all the kingdoms of the world in a moment of time, and said to him, "To you I
will give all this authority and their glory,
for it has been delivered to me, and I give
it to whom I will. If you, then, will worship me, it will all be yours." And Jesus
answered him, "It is written, 'You shall
worship the Lord your God, and him only
shall you serve.'" (Matthew 4:5–8).

Here Israel had been taken up out of Egypt but gave in
to the false gods of surrounding communities, as well as
their own golden calf. Jesus would not bow to any other
than God the Father as He referenced, "Fear the LORD
your God, serve Him only, and take your oaths in His
name" (Deuteronomy 6:13).

The final temptation came with an opportunity to reverse the test toward God.

> And he took him to Jerusalem and set him on the pinnacle of the temple and said to him, "If you are the Son of God, throw yourself down from here, for it is written, 'He will command his angels concerning you, to guard you,' and 'On their hands they will bear you up, lest you strike your foot against a stone.'" And Jesus answered him, "It is said, 'You shall not put the Lord your God to the test.'" (Matthew 4:9–12).

Israel had tested God in the wilderness, questioning whether or not He was actually with them or not. God had Moses strike a rock out of which sprang fresh water for the parched people to drink. They named the site *Massah* which means *test* to sear into memory what they had done. They literally put sin on the map.

Jesus refreshed the minds of all when we quoted "Do not test the LORD your God... as you tested Him at Massah" (Deuteronomy 6:16).

Christ did not succumb to any sin by way of the devil's temptations and thereby fulfilled the law. Christ's response was a triple emphatic of sinless perfection. Jesus then convalesced in exclusive sweet relief, attended to by angels after the diabolical ordeal.

Jesus went on and lived the perfect life, died the perfect death, only to rise victorious, forever becoming hope personified. He then appeared to numerous people during a crucial number of days, before He ascended into heaven. The Gospel writer, Luke, provides the specifics.

> "In the first book, O Theophilus, I have dealt with all that Jesus began to do and teach, until the day when he was taken up, after he had given commands through the Holy Spirit to the apostles whom he had chosen. He presented himself alive to them after his suffering by many proofs, appearing to them during forty days and speaking about the kingdom of God" (Acts 1:1–3).

It would seem more testing and hope is upon the church as we await Christ's final return.

+++

Many Christians to this day annually reflect on the suffering of Christ during the season of Lent—a forty-day observance. It is a spiritual journey toward the passion of Christ, His death and resurrection. Oftentimes, an element of fasting is incorporated into the Lenten experience, so one suffers while going without. Ideally, personal suffering is steered toward reflection on Christ's suffering and sacrifice for all. Repentance and forgiveness play a large role through this forty-day "wilderness" experience culminating in the hope in Jesus's resurrection.

Consequently, each Sunday is a mini-Easter resurrection celebration day. As if to prove the point, the Sundays

during the season of Lent do not count toward the total forty days of fasting. Good things come to those who
wait.

Martin Luther wrote:

> "The man who then can wait and be pa-
> tient, can hope for what has been delayed,
> and love what is so contrary to it, will fi-
> nally experience that God is truthful and
> keeps His promises... But God wants that
> which He promises to be invisible and
> contrary to what we see, that we may be
> tried and trained to learn the true and
> most God-pleasing worship—to await His
> time. Therefore, admonitions such as this
> are so common in the Psalms."

Interestingly enough, in some translations of Luther's
catechism, at the end of the Confession and Absolution
section, the fortieth Psalm is referenced. Psalm 40 is not
merely about waiting or suffering, but enduring the process of long-suffering rewarded.

The opening lines of David's fortieth Psalm give poetic
voice to confession and absolution:

> "I waited patiently for the Lord; he turned
> to me and heard my cry. He lifted me out
> of the slimy pit, out of the mud and mire;
> he set my feet on a rock and gave me a
> firm place to stand. He put a new song in
> my mouth, a hymn of praise to our God.

Many will see and fear the Lord and put
their trust in him."

David most likely wrote this in his younger days.
Presumably he was on the run from Saul as an enemy of
the state, pondering when and how the present ordeal
would end. God speaks beautiful words—His words—
through the psalmist's fortieth entry, directing us to confession and absolution.

This too shall pass. Whatever our present diabolical
dilemma, when we get desperate and finally are compelled to confess our sins once again, eventually we turn
to God. When all else is out of our control, waiting on
God to move and act, to deliver us from the myriad of
calamities that vex us, Christ's vindicating forgiveness ultimately and mercifully arrives. We are rescued. The test
is over. The relationship is restored. The illness subsides,
the appetite is back. The money comes through, the fi-
nancial problem solved. The cancer is gone. The storm
has passed.

The biblical usage of the number forty can help us remember how God allows us to be tested, and leads us to
hope in Him, through the process of confession and absolution. For this sinner too shall pass; from death to life,
from sin to grace, from this world to the next, through the
gates of heaven, for all of eternity. Amen!

QUESTIONS

1. Why did Israel wander in the desert for forty years?

2. Why did Jonah struggle so much with his assignment?

3. How are confession and absolution like death and resurrection?

4. Why did Jesus enter the wilderness?

5. How does the forty-day season of Lent serve you?

6. What is the significance of Ascension Day?

MEMORY

3	Three	Trinity	The Apostles Creed	The 3 Articles
7	Seven	Perfection	The Lord's Prayer	The 7 Petitions
8	Eight	Promise	Baptism	8th Day Creation
10	Ten	Completion	The Decalogue	10 Commandments
12	Twelve	The Church	Holy Communion	12 Tribes/ Apostles
40	Forty	Testing & Hope	Confession & Absolution	40 Days of Lent

CONCLUSION

Martin Luther, one of the great time-tested students of the Bible, ultimately became one of its best instructors. He possessed a strong desire for the Word of God to be readily accessible, and ideally for all people to be counted among the righteous. He was personally aware of the painful effects of the inaccessibility of the Scriptures and a veiled understanding of the Bible. The result was a strong sense of fearful dread toward an apparently wrathful God. Luther chronically questioned where he stood before God because of his sins. He even inflicted physical self-punishment in attempts to appease God. Luther's attempts of living under God's Law to perfection were as much exhausting as they were hopelessly depressing.

Not until Martin Luther painstakingly studied the Scriptures in its original languages did he recognize the Gospel and experience an epiphany. This good news of the discovery of the Gospel changed everything. God no longer seemed angry and vengeful to Luther, but just as loving and forgiving as He was powerful. The fear of death had been swallowed up in the promises of eternal life. Luther yearned for all people to see the relief and joy that is only known living under the grace of Christ's death and resurrection. The spark of the Reformation had ignited.

Two formidable obstructions were evident to him. If the doctrinal dilemma with the Roman Catholic Church wasn't menacing enough to begin, the other less obvious barrier was the lack of biblical education of the people. Few people could read the Bible, and fewer still owned one. How would the common man come to understand the finest theology and appreciate it with eternal salvific results? Fortunately, Luther was no common man. He was a monster of a reformer, ready to break through the prohibiting blockades.

Luther would go on to produce voluminous theological writings, theses, letters, essays, papers, sermons, and hymns. In time, Luther would translate the Bible from Greek into German, the language of his people. The modern technology of Gutenberg's printing press serendipitously ensured much of Luther's writings received widespread distribution. Additionally, Luther's friend and resident artist, Lucas Cranach, painted Lutheran theology to life with vivid images for the people to ponder. Meanwhile, his hymnody was sung with ever-growing vim in churches throughout the land.

Luther still was not satisfied. He desired every confessing Christian to have a firm grasp of the Bible basics. Moreover, he emphasized it was the duty of every household to instruct its children in the faith. The result was *Luther's Small Catechism*. The catechism taught at minimum, every believing Christian should be able to articulate six essential doctrinal truths as expressed in the Scriptures: The Ten Commandments, the Lord's Prayer, the Apostles' Creed, Baptism, Confession and

Absolution, and Holy Communion. These particular six doctrines would become known as the six chief parts of Luther's *Small Catechism*.

Christians for the past five centuries have been reading, studying, and memorizing the six chief parts of the catechism in various forms as a rite of passage to confirm their faith in Christianity. Maintaining these bedrock beliefs of the faith in the forefront of our minds is an ever-increasing challenge in a world hell-bent on rejecting and denying them.

Yet, we can easily remember phone numbers, social security numbers, and zip codes, and the respective identities to which those numbered sequences lead. Perhaps we could also commit to memory some of the more popular biblical numbers: 3, 7, 8, 10, 12, and 40 and the identity of our Savior, Jesus, to whom they point, along with some of His most vital teachings.

Connecting the significance of God's broad brushstroke use of biblical numbers to these specific doctrinal components will ideally be one more arrow in the quiver for any student of the Scriptures. It can be another aid to help, read, mark, learn, and inwardly digest the truth of God's Word, timelessly serving the Christian disciple. For lest we forget, possessing a firm understanding of these six chief parts of the catechism, is not a finish line for doctrinal understanding, but merely a beginning.

ACKNOWLEDGMENTS

I would like to personally thank Rick Bates, who recognized the value of the material and gave it the classic green light treatment. Also, I offer a major kudos to the creative team at Crosslink Publishing, their attention to detail and passion for their craft.

I offer a tip of the proverbial hat toward Robert Wilson, for the consummate literary agent he is, and for his noble advocacy, diligent work, and friendship.

A large debt of gratitude goes to Dr. Michael Walcheski, my Director of Christian Education during my early formative years, for gifting me with a creative approach to confirmation and catechesis. Also to Rev. Timothy Seeber, a buttressing force of pastoral leadership in my life.

A cheer of appreciation also goes to Rev. Gregory Walton, as a classy advocate and bishop, who encouraged me early on to move forward with this project.

Major thanks is in order for Rev. Dr. Dale Meyer, who was brilliantly at the helm during my seminary days as a model leader and theologian exemplar. I am also thankful for all endorsers of this book, for your time, energy, and kind words.

Unmeasured gratefulness goes to my wife, Kara—for her constant support, love, and constructively critical eye in the early editing sessions, and to our family.

And the last shall be first, to Christ Jesus, my Lord. *Soli Deo Gloria.*

REFERENCES

Brighton, Louis A. 1999. *Concordia Commentary— Revelation*, St. Louis, MO: Concordia Publishing House,.

Gibbs, Jeffery A. 2006. *Concordia Commentary—Matthew 1:1–11:1*. St. Louis, MO: Concordia Publishing House.

Gibbs, Jeffery A. 2010. *Concordia Commentary—Matthew 11:2–20:34*. St. Louis, MO: Concordia Publishing House.

Just, Arthur A. 1997. *Concordia Commentary—Luke*. St. Louis: MO: Concordia Publishing House.

Kolb, Robert, and Wengert, Timothy J. 2000. *The Book of Concord*. MN: Fortress Press.

Lessing, Reed. 2007. *Concordia Commentary—Jonah* St. Louis, MO: Concordia Publishing House.

Lockwood, Gregory J. 2000. *Concordia Commentary—1 Corinthians*. St. Louis, MO: Concordia Publishing House.

Luther, Martin. 2017. *Luther's Small Catechism with Explanation*. St. Louis, MO: Concordia Publishing House.

Luther, Martin. 1967. *Table Talk*, Luther's Works Vol. 54. Philadelphia, PA: Fortress Press.

Petersen, David. 2006. *Fusion: Numbers.* St. Louis, MO: Concordia Publishing House.

Plass, Ewald M. 1994. *What Luther Says.* (10th printing). St. Louis, MO: Concordia Publishing House.

Roehrs, Walter R., and Franzmann, Martin H. 1979. *Concordia Self-Study Commentary.* St. Louis, MO: Concordia Publishing House .

Saint Ambrose. *Letter to Horontianus.*

Saint Augustine. *Confessions* (Lib 1, 1–2, 2.5, 5:CSEL 33, 1–5).

Saint Irenaeus. *Against Heretics,* Book II 24.

Saint Justin. *Horotary Address to the Greeks.*

Steinmann, Andrew E. 2008. *Concordia Commentary—Daniel.* St. Louis, MO: Concordia Publishing House.

ABOUT THE AUTHOR

Eric T. Eichinger is an award-winning author for his previous work on *The Final Race: The Incredible WWII Story of the Olympian Who Inspired Chariots of Fire*. He graduated from Michigan State University (B.A.) where he also ran varsity track and field. He graduated from Concordia Seminary (M.Div.) before entering the pastoral office. Prior to his theological studies, Eric spent two years in China as an oral English professor where he eventually met his wife, Kara. They have three children together and reside in the Tampa Bay area. Currently, Eric serves as Senior Pastor of Bethel Lutheran Church in Clearwater, FL.

Printed in the United States
by Baker & Taylor Publisher Services